United Nations Department
for Disarmament Affairs

The United Nations and Disarmament: 1945-1985

United Nations
New York, 1985

106 116

UNITED NATIONS PUBLICATION

Sales No. E.85.IX.6

C 02295
P 01695

ISBN 92-1-142112-8

CONTENTS

iii

Chapter VIII

Chapter IX

Chapter X

Chapter XI

ACRONYMS AND ABBREVIATIONS

ABM	anti-ballistic missile
ASBM	air-to-surface ballistic missile
CCD	Conference of the Committee on Disarmament (1969-1978)*
CDE	Conference on Confidence- and Security-building Measures and Disarmament in Europe
CSCE	Conference on Security and Co-operation in Europe
ENDC	Eighteen-Nation Committee on Disarmament (1962-1968)*
EURATOM	European Atomic Energy Community
IAEA	International Atomic Energy Agency
ICBM	intercontinental ballistic missile
ISMA	international satellite monitoring agency
LRTNF	long-range theatre nuclear forces
MIRV	multiple independently targetable re-entry vehicles
NATO	North Atlantic Treaty Organization
NGO	non-governmental organization
OAU	Organization of African Unity
OPANAL	Agency for the Prohibition of Nuclear Weapons in Latin America
PGM	precision-guided munition
SALT	Strategic Arms Limitation Talks
SIPRI	Stockholm International Peace Research Institute
SLBM	submarine-launched ballistic missile
UNIDIR	United Nations Institute for Disarmament Research
WHO	World Health Organization

---

* The name of the multilateral negotiating body in Geneva was changed to Committee on Disarmament in 1979 and to Conference on Disarmament in 1984.

INTRODUCTION

Forty years ago, the United Nations was established with the basic aims of saving "succeeding generations from the scourge of war" and promoting international peace and security "with the least diversion for armaments of the world's human and economic resources". Since then, the United Nations has dealt with the increasingly complex issues concerning arms limitation and disarmament and continues to play a central role in this field.

Concern over the arms race is increasing in the international community. During the last four decades, the world's arsenals have grown to the point where the threat of a holocaust casts a shadow over everyone's life. World expenditures for military purposes have exceeded the estimated level of $800 billion a year and are expected to reach $1 trillion well before 1990. Notwithstanding both bilateral and multilateral disarmament efforts, the arms race has continued unabated.

The fortieth anniversary of the United Nations presents an opportunity to review and reflect on the period since its founding. This booklet, *The United Nations and Disarmament: 1945-1985*, sets out a broad historical overview of actions taken and efforts made in the field of arms limitation and disarmament from the creation of the Organization up to the end of March 1985. As such, the publication does not and cannot pretend to offer an exhaustive account of all the work in the field, but it is intended to provide a starting-point for any further study of the subject-matter.

Previous publications of this type have included *The United Nations versus the Arms Race* (1980) and *The United Nations and Disarmament: 1945-1970* (1970). The current booklet updates and revises those two publications on the role of the United Nations in the field of disarmament and at the same time responds to a proposal made in the United Nations, most recently at the 1985 session of the Disarmament Commission, calling for a book on United Nations disarmament efforts during the 40-year period since its founding.

The United Nations and Disarmament: 1945-1985 is published within the framework of the World Disarmament Campaign, which was launched in 1982 by a unanimous decision at the second special session of the General Assembly devoted to disarmament and which aims at informing, educating and generating public understanding and support for the objectives of the United Nations in the field of arms limitation and disarmament. The Campaign is directed to the world's population at

ix

large, but focuses on five major constituencies with a multiplier effect within society, namely, non-governmental organizations, the media, educational institutions, research institutes and elected representatives.

The publication of information materials constitutes one of the major activities of the World Disarmament Campaign as it attempts to provide balanced, objective and factual information on disarmament questions. It is hoped that this publication will be helpful in giving a historical perspective on disarmament efforts within the United Nations as well as information on the arms race, thus encouraging greater understanding and involvement in disarmament matters on the part of all the World Disarmament Campaign's constituencies.

Chapter I

The role of the United Nations in the field of disarmament

"To save succeeding generations from the scourge of war" was certainly the most profound ideal that inspired the founders of the United Nations. Meeting in San Francisco on 26 June 1945 to sign the Charter, they consistently proclaimed the maintenance of international peace and security as one of the major objectives of the Organization. The Charter accordingly prohibits the use or threat of use of force in international relations (Article 2, paragraph 4), provides for the peaceful settlement of international disputes (Chapter VI) and elaborates a mechanism for action of the Organization with regard to threats to peace, breaches of the peace and acts of aggression (Chapter VII).

Those provisions established the necessary general legal and political framework for the promotion of the cause of disarmament and, through the years, have determined the special role of the United Nations in pursuing that goal. Specific responsibilities were then conferred on the Security Council and the General Assembly in connection with disarmament and the regulation of armaments.

The General Assembly is empowered to consider "principles governing disarmament and the regulation of armaments" and to make "recommendations with regard to such principles to the Members or to the Security Council or to both" (Article 11). The Security Council, "in order to promote the establishment and maintenance of international peace and security with the least diversion for armaments of the world's human and economic resources", is responsible for formulating, with the assistance of the Military Staff Committee (Article 47), "plans to be submitted to the Members of the United Nations for the establishment of a system for the reduction of armaments" (Article 26).

Efforts between 1945 and 1978

As a result of the discovery of atomic energy and of the use of the first atomic weapons, the question of disarmament and the regulation of armaments was recognized as urgent and given due prominence. In 1946, the General Assembly established an Atomic Energy Commission, which was entrusted with the task of formulating plans to ensure that such energy would only be used for peaceful purposes. To that end the United States proposed the creation of an international atomic development

1

authority entrusted with all phases of the development and use of atomic energy. According to the proposal, once a system of control and sanctions was effectively operating, further production of atomic weapons would cease, existing stocks would be destroyed and all technological information would be communicated to the authority (Baruch Plan). The USSR, for its part, proposed a draft convention which would prohibit the production and use of atomic weapons and would provide for the destruction of all atomic weapons within three months from its entry into force (Gromyko Plan).

Subsequently, in 1947, another body for disarmament negotiations, the Commission for Conventional Armaments, was established by the decision of the Security Council. It was called upon to submit to the Council proposals for the general reduction of armaments and armed forces and for practical and effective safeguards in connection with the general regulation and reduction of armaments.

Because of substantial differences of approach between the Western Powers and the Soviet Union on the issues under consideration, including the question of verification, and a general deterioration of the international situation, the two Commissions were unable to make progress in their work. In 1952, in an attempt to break the impasse, the General Assembly decided to consolidate them into a single Disarmament Commission. The new Commission, composed of the members of the Security Council and Canada, remained the primary disarmament body until 1957. Its main objective was the preparation of proposals for the regulation, limitation and balanced reduction by stages of all armed forces and all armaments in a co-ordinated, comprehensive programme. Such proposals were also to include measures for the elimination of all major weapons adaptable to mass destruction and for effective international control of atomic energy to ensure the prohibition of atomic weapons and the use of atomic energy for peaceful purposes only.

Various views were expressed on all substantive issues placed before the Commission. Since the differences between the two sides proved insurmountable, in 1954, the Commission, acting on the suggestion of the General Assembly, created a sub-committee consisting of Canada, France, the Soviet Union, the United Kingdom and the United States and entrusted it with the task of searching for agreement on a comprehensive and co-ordinated plan of disarmament. While the four Western States placed particular emphasis on the limitation and reduction of conventional armaments and armed forces with an appropriate control system, the Soviet Union expressed interest in an early discontinuance of nuclear-weapon tests and an undertaking not to use nuclear weapons. Because of the lack of progress towards agreement on a co-ordinated, comprehensive programme, attention gradually shifted towards various partial measures that might be implemented prior to reaching agreement on such a comprehensive plan. The Disarmament Commission was enlarged in 1957 and again in 1958, the latter time to include all the Members of the United Nations. Attempts in 1958 to reconvene it were unsuccessful, however, and in fact, it held only two further sessions, in 1960 and in 1965.

Starting in 1959, the United Nations began to pursue disarmament efforts through two distinct, yet parallel, approaches. The General Assembly, acknowledging the need to concentrate on more far-reaching objectives, placed on its agenda an item entitled "General and complete disarmament under effective international control". As a result, collateral measures of disarmament that commanded broad support came to be seen as integral parts of the process of attaining the far-reaching goal, and no longer in conflict with it. Consequently, agreements on partial disarmament measures were pursued concurrently with the effort to elaborate plans for general and complete disarmament.

At the same time, disarmament matters were given renewed impetus within the bilateral framework. This was also reflected in the changes introduced in the disarmament machinery. Thus, following a decision of the foreign ministers of France, the Soviet Union, the United Kingdom and the United States, in 1959 the Ten-Nation Committee on Disarmament was established, with East and West represented in equal numbers. Its negotiating function was reorganized in 1962 with the establishment of the Eighteen-Nation Committee on Disarmament (ENDC), as a result of an agreement between the USSR and the US endorsed by the General Assembly. The ENDC, which held its first conference that year, added eight non-aligned members to the original ten. It then became the Conference of the Committee on Disarmament (CCD) in 1969, when the membership was expanded to 26 nations. The membership was expanded once again, to 31, in 1975.

Despite the fact that several important agreements for the regulation and limitation of armaments had been concluded, they were not sufficient to curb the arms race in all its aspects, and global expenditures on arms and armed forces continued to mount. Recognizing the pressing need to slow and reverse the world-wide arms race, in 1969 the General Assembly proclaimed the 1970s as the First Disarmament Decade. In particular, the Assembly called upon Governments to intensify their efforts to achieve effective measures relating to the cessation of the nuclear arms race, to nuclear disarmament and to the elimination of non-nuclear weapons of mass destruction, and to conclude a treaty on general and complete disarmament under effective international control. It recommended further that consideration be given to channelling a substantial part of the resources freed by disarmament measures towards the promotion of the economic development of developing countries. It also requested the Secretary-General and Governments to publicize the Disarmament Decade by all appropriate means at their disposal in order to acquaint public opinion with its purposes and objectives.

In 1975, the General Assembly decided to examine the role of the United Nations in the field of disarmament, primarily with a view to

3

strengthening that role. It invited all States to communicate to the Secretary-General their views and suggestions on the issue and established a specific *Ad Hoc* Committee on the Review of the Role of the United Nations in the Field of Disarmament. The review focused on the following objectives:

(*a*) New approaches to achieve more effective procedures for organizing work in the field of disarmament in order to enable the United Nations to exercise its full role in multilateral disarmament efforts;

(*b*) Ways and means of improving United Nations facilities for the collection, compilation and dissemination of information on disarmament issues in order to keep Governments as well as world public opinion informed on progress in the field;

(*c*) Ways and means of enabling the Secretariat to assist, on request, States parties to multilateral agreements in their duty to ensure their effective functioning.

As an accompanying measure, the unit of the United Nations Secretariat dealing with disarmament matters, the Disarmament Affairs Division, was enlarged and its status enhanced, as of 1 January 1977, to become the Centre for Disarmament within the Department of Political and Security Council Affairs.

First special session of the General Assembly devoted to disarmament

In line with the desire of the Organization to strengthen its role in the field of disarmament, in 1976 the General Assembly, at the initiative of the non-aligned countries and with widespread support from other Member States, decided to hold a special session devoted entirely to disarmament. Though some partial results had been achieved in the field of disarmament, they were very limited in terms of the desired arms limitation and disarmament measures. As the Secretary-General said at the opening of the special session: "These accomplishments are dwarfed by the magnitude of what remains to be done."

It was clear that no real progress had been made on halting the arms race. World military expenditures were then estimated to be at the level of $400 billion a year. While the nuclear-weapon States and other major military Powers accounted for a large portion of those expenditures, the military spending of countries outside the two main military alliances was also rising. Both quantitative and qualitative improvements of existing nuclear and conventional stockpiles had continued at an ever-increasing pace. In addition, from the end of the Second World War to the mid-1970s, more than 100 wars had been fought with conventional weapons with many millions killed.

The arms race was thus becoming more dangerous, more complex and increasingly a world-wide phenomenon. A United Nations expert

4

group declared in a 1977 report, entitled *Economic and Social Consequences of the Arms Race and of Military Expenditures*, that "the world has long since reached the point where security can only be sought in disarmament and in the expansion of international co-operation among all countries in all fields".

The convening of the special session was therefore intended to set a new course in international affairs and turn States away from the nuclear and conventional arms race by means of agreement on a global strategy for the future course of disarmament.

The first special session of the General Assembly devoted to disarmament was held in New York from 23 May to 30 June 1978. It was the largest, most representative meeting of nations ever gathered to consider the question of disarmament. All Member States participated in the work of the session and representatives of 126 of them, including 19 heads of State or Government, 51 foreign ministers and many other high-ranking officials, took part in the general debate and submitted views and ideas covering the whole range of disarmament matters.

For the first time in the history of disarmament negotiations, the international community of States achieved consensus agreement on a comprehensive disarmament strategy, embodied in the Final Document of the session, which was to be considered the guideline of all future disarmament efforts within and outside the United Nations.

The Final Document of the session pointed out that the United Nations has a central role and primary responsibility in the field of disarmament. It also contained specific measures intended to strengthen the machinery that dealt with disarmament issues within the United Nations system. Composed of four sections, namely, "Introduction", "Declaration", "Programme of Action" and "Machinery", the Final Document set out goals, principles and priorities in the field of disarmament.

The *Introduction* recognized that "the attainment of the objective of security, which is an inseparable element of peace, has always been one of the most profound aspirations of humanity. States have for a long time sought to maintain their security through the possession of arms." It stated, however, that "the accumulation of weapons, particularly nuclear weapons, today constitutes much more a threat than a protection for the future of mankind." "The time has therefore come," it continued, "to put an end to this situation, to abandon the use of force in international relations and to seek security in disarmament, that is to say, through a gradual but effective process beginning with a reduction in the present level of armaments" (paragraph 1). The *Introduction* established that "while the final objective of the efforts of all States should continue to be general and complete disarmament under effective international control, the immediate goal is that of the elimination of the danger of a nuclear war and the implementation of measures to halt and reverse the arms race and clear the path towards lasting peace" (paragraph 8).

5

The *Declaration*, whose aim was to review and assess the existing situation as well as to outline the objectives, priorities, tasks and principles for disarmament negotiations, made explicit references to the interrelationship between international security and disarmament. The *Declaration* stated that "genuine and lasting peace can only be created through the effective implementation of the security system provided for in the Charter of the United Nations and the speedy and substantial reduction of arms and armed forces, by international agreement and mutual example, leading ultimately to general and complete disarmament under effective international control" (paragraph 13). Furthermore, it pointed out that "the principal goals of disarmament are to ensure the survival of mankind and to eliminate the danger of war, in particular nuclear war, to ensure that war is no longer an instrument for settling international disputes and that the use and the threat of force are eliminated from international life, as provided for in the Charter of the United Nations" (paragraph 19). In addition, reaffirming their full commitment to the purposes of the Charter of the United Nations and their obligation strictly to observe its principles, Member States "stress[ed] the special importance of refraining from the threat or use of force against the sovereignty, territorial integrity or political independence of any State, or against peoples under colonial or foreign domination seeking to exercise their right to self-determination and to achieve independence; non-intervention and non-interference in the internal affairs of other States; the inviolability of international frontiers; and the peaceful settlement of disputes, having regard to the inherent right of States to individual and collective self-defence in accordance with the Charter" (paragraph 26).

The *Declaration* also contained a number of important principles, one of which states that "the adoption of disarmament measures should take place in such an equitable and balanced manner as to ensure the right of each State to security and to ensure that no individual State or group of States may obtain advantages over others at any stage. At each stage the objective should be undiminished security at the lowest possible level of armaments and military forces" (paragraph 29). The *Declaration* also made clear that "disarmament and arms limitation agreements should provide for adequate measures of verification satisfactory to all parties concerned in order to create the necessary confidence and ensure that they are being observed by all parties" (paragraph 31).

The *Programme of Action* set out the priorities and the measures that States should undertake as a matter of urgency in the field of disarmament: "Priorities in disarmament negotiations shall be: nuclear weapons; other weapons of mass destruction, including chemical weapons; conventional weapons including any which may be deemed to be excessively injurious or to have indiscriminate effects; and reduction of armed forces" (paragraph 45). The *Programme of Action* also enumerated a number of specific measures to be pursued in various areas.

6

The last section, *Machinery*, noted the urgency of revitalizing the existing disarmament machinery and outlined the consensus agreement reached on the establishment of appropriate forums, with a more representative character, for disarmament negotiations and deliberations as well as other activities to be undertaken. (See chapter II.)

In order to facilitate the attainment of the objectives set forth in the Final Document, in 1979 the General Assembly declared the 1980s as the Second Disarmament Decade. The new *Declaration* stated that the goals of the Decade should remain consistent with the ultimate objective of the disarmament process: general and complete disarmament under effective international control. The goals themselves were the halting and reversing of the arms race; the conclusion of agreements on disarmament according to objectives and priorities of the Final Document; the strengthening of international peace and security in keeping with the Charter of the United Nations; and the reallocation of resources from military to developmental purposes, particularly in favour of the developing countries.

In the four years following the special session, the international situation deteriorated in several important respects. The level of global military expenditures increased. A noticeable lack of confidence, also related to a disregard of the provisions of the Charter on non-use or threat of use of force in international relations, began to affect the disarmament scene negatively, particularly in the late 1970s. After some initial progress, the negotiating process stalled on virtually all the important disarmament issues. As a result, the *Programme of Action* laid down in the 1978 Final Document remained largely unimplemented.

Second special session of the General Assembly devoted to disarmament

The second special session of the General Assembly devoted to disarmament was held in New York from 7 June to 10 July 1982. The Assembly was addressed by 18 heads of State or Government and 44 foreign ministers. Altogether, more than 140 States took part in the general debate, putting forward their positions on questions of disarmament, peace and security and expressing concern over the clear lack of progress.

Over 3,000 representatives from 450 non-governmental organizations in 47 countries around the world also attended the session, and representatives of 53 non-governmental organizations and 22 research institutions made statements. In addition, thousands of communications, petitions and appeals with many millions of signatures were received by the United Nations from organizations, groups and individuals all over the world.

Over 60 proposals and position papers by Member States were circulated dealing with such questions as nuclear disarmament and prevention of war, the banning of chemical weapons, the reduction of military budgets, regional disarmament, the verification of disarmament agreements, the relationship between disarmament and development, confidence-building measures and the strengthening of the role of the United Nations in the field of disarmament. Five draft resolutions were put before the Assembly containing various proposals in the area of nuclear weapons, but general agreement was not reached on any of those proposals and none was actually put to a vote. In contrast to its experience at the first special session in 1978, the Assembly was unable to reach consensus on any specific course of action.

The second special session convened at a time of continued international tension coupled with armed conflicts in various parts of the world, in an atmosphere generally unfavourable to the reaching of agreement on matters of utmost sensitivity to the perceived national security interests of Member States.

In the Concluding Document of the session, however, the General Assembly categorically and unanimously reaffirmed the validity of the 1978 Final Document. It expressed its profound preoccupation over the danger of war, particularly nuclear war, and urged Member States to consider as soon as possible proposals designed to secure its avoidance. The Assembly stressed the need for further strengthening the role of the United Nations in the field of disarmament and enhancing the effectiveness of the disarmament machinery.

The Assembly was also able to agree on two items, namely, the launching of the World Disarmament Campaign and the continuation and expansion of the United Nations programme of fellowships on disarmament (see chapter XIII).

The Concluding Document also made reference to the holding of a third special session of the General Assembly devoted to disarmament. Resolutions adopted in 1983 and 1984 on the subject indicated that a decision would be taken by the Assembly at its fortieth session, in 1985, and that the special session itself should be convened not later than 1988.

Arms limitation and disarmament agreements

Since the inception of the United Nations, the combined efforts of Governments, both multilateral and bilateral, particularly within the various existing disarmament bodies and through regional arrangements, have resulted in limited yet significant agreements on various arms limitation and disarmament measures. The full texts of multilateral agreements concluded so far are reproduced in the 1982 United Nations publication *Status of Multilateral Arms Regulation and Disarmament Agreements*. Those agreements are:

—The 1959 *Antarctic Treaty* provides for the demilitarization of Antarctica and is the first treaty to put into practice the concept of the nuclear-weapon-free zone, later applied to Latin America, the sea-bed and outer space. Moreover, it prohibits in the Antarctic region any military manœuvres, weapon tests, building of installations or disposal of radioactive wastes produced by military activities (see chapter VII);

— The 1963 *Treaty Banning Nuclear Weapon Tests in the Atmosphere, in Outer Space and under Water* (partial test-ban Treaty) is a partial measure in that it bans nuclear tests in the atmosphere, in outer space and under water, but does not ban tests underground (see chapter V);

— The 1967 *Treaty on Principles Governing the Activities of States in the Exploration and Use of Outer Space, including the Moon and Other Celestial Bodies* (outer space Treaty) bans nuclear and other weapons of mass destruction from the Earth's orbit, prohibits the military use of celestial bodies or the placing of nuclear weapons on those bodies and bars the stationing of weapons in outer space (see chapter IX);

— The 1967 *Treaty for the Prohibition of Nuclear Weapons in Latin America* (Treaty of Tlatelolco) created the first nuclear-weapon-free zone in a densely populated area and was the first arms limitation agreement to provide for verification by an international organization (see chapter VII);

— The 1968 *Treaty on the Non-Proliferation of Nuclear Weapons* (non-proliferation Treaty) prohibits not only transfer to, but also acquisition by, non-nuclear-weapon countries of nuclear weapons; ensures access to nuclear technology for peaceful purposes and commits the nuclear-weapon States parties to pursue in good faith negotiations on effective measures relating to cessation of the nuclear arms race and to nuclear disarmament;

— The 1971 *Treaty on the Prohibition of the Emplacement of Nuclear Weapons and Other Weapons of Mass Destruction on the Sea-Bed and the Ocean Floor and in the Subsoil Thereof* (sea-bed Treaty) bans the placement of nuclear and other weapons of mass destruction and facilities for such weapons on or under the sea-bed outside a 12-mile coastal zone referred to in the 1958 Geneva Convention on the Territorial Sea and the Contiguous Zone (see chapter VII);

— The 1972 *Convention on the Prohibition of the Development, Production and Stockpiling of Bacteriological (Biological) and Toxin Weapons and on Their Destruction* (biological weapons Convention) is the first international agreement providing for a genuine measure of disarmament, that is, the complete elimination of one category of existing weapons (see chapter VIII);

— The 1977 *Convention on the Prohibition of Military or Any Other Hostile Use of Environmental Modification Techniques* (ENMOD Convention) prohibits the use of techniques that would have widespread, long-lasting or severe effects in causing such phenomena as earthquakes, tidal waves and changes in weather and climate patterns (see chapter X);

9

— The 1979 *Agreement Governing the Activities of States on the Moon and Other Celestial Bodies* (Agreement on celestial bodies) prohibits, *inter alia*, the use of the Moon and other celestial bodies for military purposes (see chapter IX);

— The 1981 *Convention on Prohibitions or Restrictions on the Use of Certain Conventional Weapons Which May Be Deemed to Be Excessively Injurious or to Have Indiscriminate Effects* (Convention on inhumane weapons) restricts or prohibits the use of mines and booby traps, incendiary weapons and fragments not detectable by X-ray in the human body (see chapter XI).

Over the same period, bilateral negotiations between the USSR and the United States produced a number of agreements, including:

— The 1972 *Treaty on the Limitation of Anti-Ballistic Missile Systems* (ABM Treaty), which restricts in general such systems and specifically limits deployment of ABM systems to two sites with no more than 100 launchers each. By the 1974 Protocol, the deployment of ABM systems is further limited to a single area (see SALT I in chapter IV);

— The 1972 *Interim Agreement on Certain Measures with respect to the Limitation of Strategic Offensive Arms* (Interim Agreement), which established limitations for a five-year period — which could be extended — on the number of launchers of strategic weapons (see SALT I in chapter IV);

— The 1973 *Agreement on the Prevention of Nuclear War*, by which the parties agree to make the removal of the danger of nuclear war and of the use of nuclear weapons an objective of their policies and to make all efforts towards guaranteeing stability and peace (see chapter IV);

— The 1974 *Treaty on the Limitation of Underground Nuclear-Weapon Tests* (threshold test-ban Treaty), which establishes a nuclear "threshold" by prohibiting underground nuclear-weapon tests having a yield exceeding 150 kilotons (see chapter V);

— The 1976 *Treaty on Underground Nuclear Explosions for Peaceful Purposes* (peaceful nuclear explosions Treaty), which prohibits the carrying out of any individual nuclear explosion having a yield exceeding 150 kilotons; any group explosion having an aggregate yield exceeding 1,500 kilotons and any group explosion having an aggregate yield exceeding 150 kilotons, unless the individual explosion can be identified and measured by agreed verification procedures (see chapter V);

— The 1979 *Treaty on the Limitation of Strategic Offensive Arms*, which establishes limits on the number and types of strategic nuclear delivery vehicles (see chapter IV).

The last three Treaties have not entered into force, but each party has declared its intention to adhere to the Treaties' substantive provisions as long as the other does likewise.

Chapter II

Disarmament machinery

The machinery which deals with disarmament and related international security issues within the United Nations framework was originally established by the Charter of the United Nations and subsequent decisions of the General Assembly and the Security Council. Over the years, it has undergone various changes which have reflected the prevailing circumstances in international relations at a given time, on the one hand, and have been designed to facilitate deliberations and negotiating processes, on the other. The most recent changes in the machinery took place following the first special session of the General Assembly devoted to disarmament, in 1978.

General Assembly

The Assembly is composed of the representatives of all Member States. Under the Charter, it has the mandate to consider and make recommendations on the principles of co-operation in the maintenance of international peace and security, including the principles governing disarmament and the regulation of armaments. It can also discuss and make recommendations on any question relating to international peace and security, except when a dispute or situation is currently being discussed by the Security Council. Even though the Security Council also holds specific responsibilities in the field of disarmament, since the 1950s the Assembly and its subsidiary organs have, in practice, exercised the main initiative. It is interesting to note that the very first resolution of the General Assembly, adopted on 24 January 1946, dealt with disarmament. It sought the elimination of atomic weapons and other weapons of mass destruction and the assurance that atomic energy would be used only for peaceful purposes.

According to the Final Document of the 1978 special session devoted to disarmament, the General Assembly had been and should remain the chief deliberative organ of the United Nations in the field of disarmament and should make every effort to facilitate the implementation of disarmament measures. Furthermore, it should be informed of all disarmament efforts outside its aegis without prejudice to the progress of negotiations.

In recent years, the number of disarmament resolutions adopted by the General Assembly has been steadily increasing. In 1984, out of a total

11

of 247 resolutions adopted, 63 were on disarmament matters and 8 were on related international security questions. In addition, 3 decisions were taken on disarmament matters.

The General Assembly is thus a permanent forum for disarmament deliberations and the main source of both initiatives and recommendations by the international community on the whole spectrum of disarmament-related issues.

First Committee

The First Committee, consisting of all Member States, is one of the seven Main Committees of the General Assembly and is subject to its rules of procedure. As mandated by the General Assembly at its first special session devoted to disarmament, the First Committee deals exclusively with disarmament and related international security questions. It examines disarmament and related international security questions and recommends draft resolutions to the plenary meetings of the Assembly for adoption. The First Committee holds its substantive session from October to December every year.

In 1984, the programme of work of the First Committee included, *inter alia*, the review and implementation of recommendations and decisions adopted at the first and second special sessions of the General Assembly devoted to disarmament, as well as agenda items dealing with such issues as general and complete disarmament, cessation of the nuclear arms race and nuclear disarmament, cessation of nuclear-weapon tests, prevention of nuclear war, establishment of nuclear-weapon-free zones, reduction of military budgets, chemical and bacteriological (biological) weapons, new types of weapons of mass destruction and new systems of such weapons, relationship between disarmament and development, prevention of an arms race in outer space, conclusion of an international convention on the strengthening of the security of non-nuclear-weapon States against the use or threat of use of nuclear weapons, studies on specific issues and procedural matters.

Disarmament Commission

The Disarmament Commission provides a subsidiary forum for deliberation on disarmament issues as mandated by the General Assembly, when the Assembly is not in session. It is a successor to the earlier Disarmament Commission, established in 1952, which, although active in the 1950s, did not meet after 1965.

According to the 1978 Final Document, which specifically re-established the Disarmament Commission, it is a deliberative body and a subsidiary organ of the General Assembly, whose function is to consider and make recommendations on various problems in the field of disarmament and to follow up the relevant decisions and recommendations of the special sessions devoted to disarmament.

The Disarmament Commission, like the First Committee, is composed of all Member States of the Organization. It meets in New York for a substantive session of approximately four weeks, usually in May/June, and reports annually to the General Assembly.

Since 1979, the Commission has dealt with, among other items, elements of a comprehensive programme of disarmament, various aspects of nuclear and conventional disarmament, the relationship between disarmament and development, the Declaration of the 1980s as the Second Disarmament Decade, the overall question of the reduction of military budgets, guidelines for a comprehensive study on conventional weapons, the elaboration of guidelines for confidence-building measures and the question of South Africa's nuclear capability.

Ad hoc committees

The General Assembly may decide to establish *ad hoc* committees in order to deal with specific disarmament matters. Currently and for the past several years there have been two such committees, namely, the *Ad Hoc* Committee on the World Disarmament Conference and the *Ad Hoc* Committee on the Indian Ocean.

A. *Ad Hoc* COMMITTEE ON THE WORLD DISARMAMENT CONFERENCE

In some of the early plans for general disarmament, provision was made for a world disarmament conference. In 1964, the idea arose in a new context. Meeting in Cairo in October, the heads of State or Government of non-aligned countries proposed such a conference and stressed the desirability of having all countries participate.

In 1965, the General Assembly adopted a resolution by 112 votes to none, with 1 abstention (France), which endorsed the idea of convening a world disarmament conference. That idea was revived in 1971 on the initiative of the Soviet Union, when the General Assembly adopted by consensus a resolution stating that consideration should be given to the convening, following adequate preparation, of a world disarmament conference open to all States.

In 1973, also by consensus, the General Assembly decided to establish the *Ad Hoc* Committee on the World Disarmament Conference to examine views and suggestions expressed by Governments on the holding of such a conference, including conditions for its convening.

Each year since that time, the *Ad Hoc* Committee has submitted reports to the Assembly in which it has repeatedly stated that, notwithstanding differences of viewpoint which have been hindering progress towards the convening of a world disarmament conference, there exists the possibility that, with adequate preparation and universal participation, such a conference could be a useful forum. The *Ad Hoc* Committee maintains close contact with the nuclear-weapon States in order to remain informed of their attitudes, as well as with all other States, and considers any possible relevant proposals and observations which might be made to it.

Forty non-nuclear-weapon States are members of the Committee, and pursuant to the 1973 General Assembly resolution, nuclear-weapon States are invited to co-operate or maintain contact with it and enjoy the same rights as the other members.

B. *Ad Hoc* COMMITTEE ON THE INDIAN OCEAN

In 1971, the General Assembly adopted a resolution entitled "Declaration of the Indian Ocean as a Zone of Peace". The resolution stated, *inter alia*, that the Indian Ocean, within limits to be determined, was designated for all time as a zone of peace. The resolution was adopted by a vote of 61 to none, with 55 abstentions.

The following year, the Assembly adopted another resolution by a vote of 95 to none with 33 abstentions, by which it decided to establish the *Ad Hoc* Committee on the Indian Ocean to study the implementation of the 1971 Declaration, with specific reference to the practical measures that could be taken to carry out its objectives.

Since 1980, the *Ad Hoc* Committee's main responsibility has been to make the necessary preparations for the convening of a conference on the Indian Ocean, which would consider the effective implementation of the Declaration.

The *Ad Hoc* Committee is currently composed of 48 Member States, including all the permanent members of the Security Council.

Conference on Disarmament (CD)

The Conference on Disarmament (called the Committee on Disarmament between 1979 and 1983) is, in the language of the Final Document of the first special session on disarmament, the "single multilateral disarmament negotiating forum" of the international community. Its membership of 40 States includes all 5 nuclear-weapon States and 35 other States. The Conference on Disarmament was constituted in this configuration in 1978. It held its first session in 1979 carrying forward the negotiating efforts of its predecessors, including the Ten-Nation Committee on Disarmament (1959-1960), the ENDC (1962-1969) and the CCD (1969-1978).

The Conference on Disarmament, which meets in Geneva, has a unique relationship with the United Nations. It defines its own rules of procedure and develops its own agenda, taking into account the recommendations made by the General Assembly. It also reports to the General

Assembly annually or more frequently as may be appropriate. The Secretary-General of the Conference is appointed by the Secretary-General of the United Nations, following consultations with the Conference, and also acts as his personal representative. In 1979, the Committee on Disarmament agreed on a permanent agenda consisting of ten areas:

(1) Nuclear weapons in all aspects.

(2) Chemical weapons.

(3) Other weapons of mass destruction.

(4) Conventional weapons.

(5) Reduction of military budgets.

(6) Reduction of armed forces.

(7) Disarmament and development.

(8) Disarmament and international security.

(9) Collateral measures; confidence-building measures; effective verification methods in relation to appropriate disarmament measures acceptable to all parties concerned.

(10) Comprehensive programme of disarmament leading to general and complete disarmament under effective international control.

From that so-called decalogue, the Conference on Disarmament adopts an annual agenda and programme of work. The agenda for 1985 included the following substantive items:

(1) Nuclear test ban.

(2) Cessation of the nuclear arms race and nuclear disarmament.

(3) Prevention of nuclear war, including all related matters.

(4) Chemical weapons.

(5) Prevention of an arms race in outer space.

(6) Effective international arrangements to assure non-nuclear-weapon States against the use or threat of use of nuclear weapons.

(7) New types of weapons of mass destruction and new system of such weapons; radiological weapons.

(8) Comprehensive programme of disarmament.

The Conference is in the process of considering the expansion of its membership from 40 to not more than 44 States.

United Nations Department for Disarmament Affairs

The role of the United Nations Secretariat in disarmament matters derives from the general functions of the Secretary-General as defined in the Charter and developed over the years through the decisions of the

15

General Assembly and other United Nations bodies. The Department, which is located at United Nations Headquarters in New York and which maintains a Branch in Geneva, is the organizational unit of the Secretariat dealing with disarmament matters.

Pursuant to a 1982 resolution of the General Assembly which sought to strengthen the efforts of the United Nations in the field of disarmament, the former Centre for Disarmament within the Department of Political and Security Council Affairs was transformed, on 1 January 1983, into a Department headed by an Under-Secretary-General reporting directly to the Secretary-General.

The Department consists of the Office of the Under-Secretary-General, three functional Branches, and a Co-ordination and World Disarmament Campaign Section.

The Office of the Under-Secretary-General assists the Under-Secretary-General in the formulation of policies and in the management of the work of the Department and analyses and assesses disarmament-related developments within and outside the United Nations system to facilitate policy formulation and decision-making. The *Co-ordination and World Disarmament Campaign Section*, which is a part of the Office, carries out the activities of the Department in connection with its participation in interdepartmental and inter-agency bodies; co-ordinates the World Disarmament Campaign within the United Nations system and carries out the activities assigned to the Department in that area; and maintains liaison with non-governmental organizations and other constituencies of the World Disarmament Campaign.

The Committee and Conference Services Branch provides secretariat, administrative and substantive support services to the First Committee, the Disarmament Commission, *ad hoc* committees, other working groups that may be set up by the General Assembly and its subsidiary bodies, and review conferences of parties to disarmament agreements, treaties and conventions; follows up resolutions and decisions of the General Assembly and prepares reports thereon to it; and carries out functions assigned to the Department deriving from the Secretary-General's role as depositary of certain multilateral conventions in the field of disarmament.

The Information and Studies Branch prepares United Nations publications on disarmament, arms limitation and related subjects, including recurrent publications, such as *The United Nations Disarmament Yearbook* and the periodical *Disarmament*, and non-recurrent ones, including the Fact Sheet series and the disarmament Study Series. It plans the meetings of expert groups assisting the Secretary-General with disarmament studies mandated by the General Assembly and provides secretariat and substantive support to such meetings. It maintains a library of disarmament-related materials, provides the necessary services for the

Secretary-General in the Advisory Board on Disarmament Studies and supplies data processing services.

The Geneva Branch provides secretariat, administrative and substantive support services to the Conference on Disarmament; participates, as appropriate, in the servicing of other disarmament bodies, including review conferences of existing treaties and treaty-making conferences; oversees the implementation of the United Nations programme of fellowships on disarmament; carries out regional activities of the Department in connection with the World Disarmament Campaign, as appropriate, including liaison with its non-governmental constituencies; prepares and maintains the official records and other documentation of the Conference on Disarmament and a collection of documentation and specialized literature on armaments and disarmament.

United Nations Institute for Disarmament Research (UNIDIR)

The United Nations Institute for Disarmament Research was established on 1 October 1980. It undertakes independent research on disarmament and related security issues and works in close relationship with the Department for Disarmament Affairs. The Institute is located at the Palais des Nations in Geneva and is financed within existing United Nations resources, supplemented by voluntary contributions from Governments, non-governmental organizations, foundations and individuals. UNIDIR is governed by a Board of Trustees whose composition is that of the Advisory Board on Disarmament Studies (see below), plus the Director of the Institute.

Advisory Board on Disarmament Studies

The Advisory Board on Disarmament Studies was established in 1978 by the General Assembly at its special session on disarmament to advise the Secretary-General on various aspects of studies on disarmament to be made under the auspices of the United Nations. The Board is made up of eminent persons selected by the Secretary-General on the basis of their personal expertise and according to the principle of equitable geographical representation.

Its membership includes current and former cabinet ministers, senior governmental officials, permanent representatives to the United Nations and outstanding academic personalities. The Board also serves as the Board of Trustees of UNIDIR and advises the Secretary-General on the implementation of the World Disarmament Campaign and on other questions, upon request.

Chapter III

General and complete disarmament and comprehensive programme of disarmament

General and complete disarmament

The goal of general and complete disarmament under effective international control was proclaimed by the United Nations in 1959 as the ultimate aim of disarmament efforts. An international instrument leading to that goal was to be worked out and agreed upon in the shortest possible time. A number of proposals were subsequently put forward for the reduction of armaments in stages, with variations as to which types of arms or forces would be reduced first, numerical limits to be set, time-limits and methods of verification. Despite discussions in the United Nations, in the Geneva negotiating bodies and elsewhere, no agreement has been reached on an all-inclusive plan leading to general and complete disarmament.

In a joint statement of agreed principles on disarmament, set forth by the United States and the Soviet Union in 1961, the two Powers stated that a programme for disarmament applying to all countries should provide for the disbanding of armed forces, the dismantling of military establishments, including bases, the cessation of arms production, the liquidation of armaments or their conversion to peaceful purposes, the elimination of all stockpiles of nuclear, chemical, bacteriological and other weapons of mass destruction as well as their means of delivery, the abolition of military institutions, the cessation of military training and the discontinuance of military expenditures. The statement called for creation of an international disarmament organization within the framework of the United Nations, whose inspectors would have unrestricted access to all places, as necessary, for verification of disarmament measures, and it envisaged arrangements for a United Nations peace force.

The most elaborate proposals based on that approach were the Soviet "Draft treaty on general and complete disarmament under strict international control" and the American "Outline of basic provisions of a treaty on general and complete disarmament in a peaceful world", which were submitted to the ENDC in 1962, on 15 March and 18 April respectively. Those proposals and revisions to them were discussed during the

19

following few years, but no agreement was reached due to various differences which arose between the two groups of States most centrally concerned, particularly in the area of stages of implementation, nuclear issues and verification.

The discussions and negotiations in various disarmament forums have confirmed once again that reaching agreement to begin implementation of such measures has never been and is not easily at hand. In the process, general and complete disarmament ceased to be regarded as something likely to be achieved through a single, comprehensive instrument which would specify various sequences for nuclear and conventional disarmament and define the final status for the remaining forces and armaments.

Instead, general and complete disarmament began to be regarded as a goal to work towards in the expectation that one achievement might follow upon another, in accordance with certain logical priorities, with each stage of success creating increased mutual confidence and adding to the chances of success in the next phase.

In 1978, at its first special session devoted to disarmament, the Assembly reaffirmed by consensus the goal of general and complete disarmament under effective international control. At the same time, the Final Document of the session explicitly called for the elaboration of a comprehensive programme of disarmament encompassing all measures thought to be advisable to contribute to the realization of general and complete disarmament.

Although the concept of general and complete disarmament has been consistently referred to in statements in United Nations bodies and in other conferences and negotiating forums, it is widely recognized that so far there is little real common ground that can be translated into practical action.

Comprehensive programme of disarmament

As Member States of the United Nations became aware that the ultimate goal of general and complete disarmament was difficult to attain in the near future, the emphasis in their disarmament efforts after the mid-1960s focused more and more on partial measures. However, the interest in a comprehensive approach was not abandoned. In fact, in the late 1960s it received a new impetus. In the introduction to his annual report on the work of the Organization for 1968-1969, the Secretary-General of the United Nations, U Thant, included a proposal for the designation of the 1970s as a Disarmament Decade and, in that context, expressed the view that the General Assembly could establish a specific programme and timetable for dealing with all aspects of arms limitation and disarmament. The Assembly, after having considered the idea, adopted a resolution declaring the 1970s as the First Disarmament

Decade. The Assembly, *inter alia*, requested the CCD, while continuing intensive negotiations with a view to reaching the widest possible agreement on collateral measures, to work out at the same time a comprehensive programme dealing with all aspects of the problem of the cessation of the arms race and general and complete disarmament under effective international control, which, in the words of the resolution, "would provide the Conference with a guideline to chart the course of its further work and its negotiations".

Consequently, the CCD held discussions concerning such a programme in the period between 1970 and 1978 and a number of specific proposals were submitted, including, for instance, a 1970 joint draft comprehensive programme of disarmament by Mexico, Sweden and Yugoslavia, as well as suggestions contained in working papers presented that same year by Italy and the Netherlands. At its 1970 session, the General Assembly considered various proposals on the issue and adopted a resolution recommending that the CCD take them into account in its further work and its negotiations. It was, however, only in early 1978 that the CCD was able to agree on the establishment of a working group to elaborate a draft comprehensive programme of disarmament.

Parallel to the developments in the CCD, the question of a comprehensive programme was further discussed in the General Assembly, first under the item on general and complete disarmament, which appeared each year on the agenda, and then, starting in 1975, under the item concerning the implementation of the purposes and objectives of the Disarmament Decade.

In 1978, at its first special session devoted to disarmament, the General Assembly provided a new impetus to efforts for the elaboration of a comprehensive programme of disarmament. In the *Programme of Action* of the Final Document of that session (paragraph 109), the Assembly stated:

"Implementation of these priorities should lead to general and complete disarmament under effective international control, which remains the ultimate goal of all efforts exerted in the field of disarmament. Negotiations on general and complete disarmament should be conducted concurrently with negotiations on partial measures of disarmament. With this purpose in mind, the Committee on Disarmament will undertake the elaboration of a comprehensive programme of disarmament encompassing all measures thought to be advisable in order to ensure that the goal of general and complete disarmament under effective international control becomes a reality in a world in which international peace and security prevail and in which the new international economic order is strengthened and consolidated. The comprehensive programme should contain appropriate procedures for ensuring that the General Assembly is kept fully informed of the progress of the negotiations including an appraisal of the situation when appropriate and, in particular, a continuing review of the implementation of the programme."

To provide further guidelines, the Assembly entrusted the Disarmament Commission, in paragraph 118 of the Final Document, with the task of considering the elements of a comprehensive programme of disarmament to be submitted as recommendations to the Assembly and, through it, to the Committee on Disarmament. The Assembly reaffirmed that request to the Disarmament Commission at its regular thirty-third session, the same year.

During its 1979 session, the Commission successfully fulfilled its mandate by adopting by consensus the "Elements of a comprehensive programme of disarmament". The "Elements" contained the following parts: "I. Introduction"; "II. Objectives, principles and priorities"; "III. Measures"; "IV. Machinery and procedures"; and "V. General". The substantive sections of the text read as follows:

"II. Objectives, principles and priorities

"8.   The immediate objective of a comprehensive programme of disarmament should be to maintain and further the momentum generated by the first special session of the General Assembly devoted to disarmament, to initiate and expedite urgent negotiations on halting the arms race in all its aspects, to open a process of genuine disarmament on an internationally agreed basis and to increase international confidence and relaxation of international tension.

"9.   The long-term objectives should be, through the co-ordinated implementation of the comprehensive programme of disarmament, to achieve general and complete disarmament under effective international control, to avert the danger of war and to create conditions for a just and stable international peace and security and the full realization of the new international economic order.

"10.   The elaboration of the comprehensive programme of disarmament should take place as urgently as possible and parallel with the negotiations on concrete disarmament measures, particularly those agreed in the Programme of Action adopted at the tenth special session of the General Assembly. The comprehensive programme of disarmament should contain a phased programme covering measures in the different fields in which the implementation of the first stage should effectively contribute to the halting of the arms race and to the opening of the process of genuine disarmament.

"11.   During the first stage of the implementation of the comprehensive programme of disarmament, special attention should be given to the immediate cessation of the nuclear arms race and the removal of the threat of a nuclear war.

"12.   The comprehensive programme of disarmament should be elaborated and implemented on the basis of the strict observance of the principles contained in the Final Document and in accordance with the priorities stated in paragraph 45 thereof, it being understood that nothing should preclude States from conducting negotiations on all priority items concurrently.

"III.   Measures

"13.   The process to be outlined in the comprehensive programme of disarmament should be conceived and implemented in accordance with the fundamental principles enshrined in the Final Document of the Tenth Special Session of the General Assembly. It should take place in such an equitable manner as to ensure the right of each State to security, *inter alia,* through the adoption of appropriate measures, taking into account the importance of nuclear disarmament and conventional disarmament, the special responsibility of the States with the largest military arsenals and the necessity for adequate measures of verification.

"14.   The comprehensive programme of disarmament should encompass the following measures as envisaged in the relevant paragraphs of the Final Document of the Tenth Special Session:

"A.   Disarmament measures

"1.   *Nuclear weapons*

"(*a*)   Nuclear-test ban;

"(*b*)   Cessation of the nuclear arms race in all its aspects and nuclear disarmament, which will require urgent negotiation of agreements at appropriate stages and with adequate measures of verification satisfactory to the States concerned for:

> "(i) Cessation of the qualitative improvement and development of nuclear weapon systems;
>
> "(ii) Cessation of the production of all types of nuclear weapons and their means of delivery, and the production of fissionable material for weapons purposes;
>
> "(iii) Reduction of stockpiles of nuclear weapons and their means of delivery, leading to their ultimate and complete elimination at the earliest possible time;

"(*c*)   Effective international arrangements to assure non-nuclear-weapon States against the use or threat of use of nuclear weapons;

"(*d*)   Continuation of the strategic arms limitation negotiations between the two parties concerned;

"(*e*) Further steps to prevent the spread of nuclear weapons, in accordance with the provisions of paragraphs 65 to 71 of the Final Document;

"(*f*) Establishment of nuclear-weapon-free zones.

"2. *Other weapons of mass destruction*

"(*a*) Prohibition of the development, production and stockpiling of all chemical weapons and their destruction;

"(*b*) Prevention of the emergence of new types of weapons of mass destruction and new systems of such weapons;

"(*c*) Prohibition of the development, production and use of radiological weapons.

"3. *Conventional weapons and armed forces*

"(*a*) Cessation of the conventional arms race;

"(*b*) Agreements and measures, multilateral, regional and bilateral, on the limitation and reduction of conventional weapons and armed forces;

"(*c*) Prohibitions or restrictions of use of certain conventional weapons, including those which may cause unnecessary suffering or which may have indiscriminate effects, taking into account the result of the 1979 United Nations Conference on Prohibitions or Restrictions of Use of Certain Conventional Weapons Which May Be Deemed to Be Excessively Injurious or to Have Indiscriminate Effects;

"(*d*) Consultations among major arms suppliers and recipients on the international transfer of conventional weapons.

"4. *Military expenditures*

"Reduction of military expenditures.

"5. *Verification*

"Verification methods and procedures in relation to specific disarmament measures, to facilitate the conclusion and effective implementation of disarmament agreements and to create confidence among States.

"6. *Related measures*

"(*a*) Further steps to prohibit military or any other hostile use of environmental modification techniques;

24

"(*b*) Consideration of further steps to prevent an arms race on the sea-bed and the ocean floor and the subsoil thereof;

"(*c*) Further steps to prevent an arms race in outer space;

"(*d*) Establishment of zones of peace.

"B. OTHER MEASURES

"1. Confidence-building measures, taking into account the characteristics of each region.

"2. Measures aimed at achieving relaxation of international tension.

"3. Measures aimed at preventing the use of force in international relations, subject to the provisions of the Charter of the United Nations.

"4. Implementation of the provisions contained in the Final Document intended to mobilize world public opinion in favour of disarmament.

"5. Disarmament studies under the auspices of the United Nations.

"NOTE: With reference to the measures dealt with in the present section, explicit mention was made of the following United Nations declarations:

"1. Declaration of Principles of International Law concerning Friendly Relations and Co-operation among States in accordance with the Charter of the United Nations;

"2. Declaration on the Strengthening of International Security;

"3. Declaration on the Preparation of Societies for Life in Peace.

"C. DISARMAMENT AND DEVELOPMENT

"Bearing in mind the close relationship between disarmament and development and taking into account the United Nations studies carried out in this field, the comprehensive programme of disarmament should include measures aimed at ensuring that disarmament makes an effective contribution to economic and social development and, in particular, to the full realization of the new international economic order through:

"(i) Reallocation of resources from military purposes to economic and social development, especially for the benefit of the developing countries;

"(ii) Savings from the reduction of military expenditures particularly by nuclear-weapon States and other militarily

25

significant States should increase the flow of resources to economic and social development, especially for the benefit of the developing countries;

"(iii) Strengthening of international co-operation for the promotion of the transfer and utilization of nuclear technology for economic and social development, especially in the developing countries, taking into account the provisions of paragraphs 68 to 70 of the Final Document.

"D. Disarmament and international security

"Strengthening of international procedures and institutions for:

"(i) Maintenance of peace and security in accordance with the Charter of the United Nations;

"(ii) Peaceful settlement of disputes;

"(iii) Effectiveness of the security system of the Charter of the United Nations;

"(iv) United Nations peace-keeping in conformity with the Charter of the United Nations.

"IV. Machinery and procedures

"A. Role of the United Nations

"15. (a) The United Nations should play a central role in the consideration and adoption of the comprehensive programme of disarmament. It must also play an adequate role in its implementation. It is essential, therefore, that the General Assembly and, through it, the Commission are regularly kept informed of the results of the negotiations on and elaboration of the comprehensive programme of disarmament. It is also essential that the United Nations be kept duly informed through the Assembly, or any other appropriate United Nations channel reaching all Members of the Organization, of all disarmament efforts outside its aegis without prejudice to the progress of negotiations.

"(b) Convening, as necessary, of special sessions of the United Nations General Assembly devoted to disarmament.

"(c) The United Nations should sponsor programmes to promote public awareness of the dangers of the arms race, its effects on international peace and security, its economic and social consequences and its effect on the attainment of the new international economic order.

"(d) The Secretary-General shall periodically submit reports to the General Assembly on the economic and social consequences of the armaments race and its extremely harmful effects on world peace and security.

"B. Form of negotiations

"16.   The negotiations of the measures envisaged in the comprehensive programme of disarmament can be conducted on a bilateral, regional or multilateral level, depending on how, in each case, effective disarmament agreements can most readily be achieved. The international disarmament machinery should ensure that all disarmament issues are being dealt with in an appropriate context.

"C. World Disarmament Conference

"17.   At the earliest appropriate time, a world disarmament conference should be convened with universal participation and with adequate preparation.

"D. Review and verification of agreed measures

"18.   Examination of the requirements of an institutional and procedural nature to facilitate the disarmament process and to ensure implementation of disarmament agreements, including the relevant proposals referred to in paragraph 125 of the Final Document, or made elsewhere."

The above text was submitted in 1979 to the General Assembly for its examination and transmission to the Committee on Disarmament.

In 1980, the Committee on Disarmament established an *ad hoc* working group in order to initiate negotiations on such a programme, with a view to completing its elaboration before the second special session of the General Assembly devoted to disarmament, in 1982.

An outline of the comprehensive programme of disarmament based on the recommendations of the Disarmament Commission was subsequently adopted by the *Ad Hoc* Working Group. It consisted of six sections: "Introduction or Preamble", "Objectives", "Principles", "Priorities", "Measures and stages of implementation" and "Machinery and procedures".

Although the draft indicated that agreement was achieved in certain areas, it presented many unagreed paragraphs and sentences — within brackets — which reflected serious differences of approach among various groups. Those differences centred on the main elements of the programme, i.e., measures and stages of implementation, including the question of whether the programme should specify time-frames. Differences also arose regarding machinery and procedures. In addition to substantive matters, divergent views were expressed on the "nature" of the programme, that is, what kind of commitment it would entail.

With respect to stages of implementation, the group of non-aligned and neutral countries initially proposed a four-stage programme encompassing all the measures necessary to achieve general and complete disarmament. Both China and the socialist countries supported in general terms the approach of that group. Western countries, stressing the difficulty of foreseeing the course of disarmament negotiations, maintained that the programme should specify only the measures to be achieved in the first stage and that those to be taken subsequently should be merely listed, without being assigned to a particular stage. It would then be the object of periodic reviews to determine whether a stage could be declared as concluded and what measures should be eventually pursued in the next stage.

With regard to the question of time-frames, the non-aligned and neutral countries, the socialist countries and China held that there should be a time limit for the implementation of each stage and for the programme as a whole. Readjustments, if and when necessary, could be made in periodic reviews.

On the other hand, Western countries held that it would be inappropriate to have time-frames, even if only indicative, for the implementation of measures. In their opinion, it was unrealistic to specify time-frames for the conclusion of relevant disarmament agreements, since their negotiation was a difficult process and dependent on unpredictable factors. They felt that the reviews of implementation to be carried out at periodic intervals would give impetus for continued progress towards the realization of the comprehensive programme itself.

The kind of commitment that such a programme would entail was also envisaged in different ways. Most members were of the view that while the programme should, in one way or another, embody a firm commitment to its implementation, it could not constitute a legally binding document. Some non-aligned States, however, believed that the programme should be of a legally binding nature, with some suggesting that it be embodied in an instrument and others favouring its adoption in formal declarations by heads of State.

At the second special session of the General Assembly devoted to disarmament, in 1982, an *ad hoc* working group was established in order to proceed with the elaboration of the comprehensive programme on the basis of the draft submitted by the Committee on Disarmament. However, the differences outlined above persisted throughout the special session, and no agreement could be reached on a revised draft.

In the Concluding Document of the special session, the Assembly recorded its decision to refer the draft programme back to the Committee on Disarmament and requested it to submit a revised draft at the

Assembly's 1983 session. Accordingly, the Committee re-established its *Ad Hoc* Working Group on the Comprehensive Programme.

Later in 1983, the Committee transmitted to the General Assembly a shorter and more modest programme than that originally envisaged. The General Assembly, while welcoming the progress achieved, also noted that the programme submitted to it needed further elaboration to reflect the broad scope of paragraph 109 of the Final Document. It therefore urged the Conference on Disarmament to renew its work on the programme when the circumstances were propitious and to present a complete draft to it not later than 1986. The Conference was also requested to submit a progress report at its 1984 session.

In 1984, the Conference on Disarmament again re-established the subsidiary body — now the *Ad Hoc* Committee on the question — with the mandate to submit to the General Assembly the complete draft of the programme, but no substantive progress was made. The Conference expressed the hope that early the following year circumstances would permit the resumption of work on the elaboration of the programme and its successful conclusion. The General Assembly, for its part, once again urged the Conference to make all efforts to submit a complete draft of the comprehensive programme of disarmament to it in 1986 and requested a progress report in 1985.

Chapter IV

Nuclear disarmament

A few weeks after the signing of the United Nations Charter, the first atomic bombs were exploded. Their immense destructive power confronted the world with military and political problems of unprecedented magnitude.

Today there are some 50,000 nuclear warheads deployed worldwide on the territories of the nuclear-weapon States and some non-nuclear-weapon States, as well as on the high seas.

In 1945 only the United States had the technology to produce nuclear weapons, but within a few years the Soviet Union (1949) developed a nuclear capability, followed later by the United Kingdom (1952), France (1960) and China (1964). The original atomic or fission bomb was followed by the more potent hydrogen or thermonuclear fusion bomb.

According to a United Nations study on nuclear weapons, technological advances have made it possible for one nuclear weapon to release in one microsecond more energy than the total amount released from all conventional weapons in all wars in history. Until the early 1960s, the tendency had been to develop ever more powerful weapons. Since then, the trend has been towards more compact weapons, but even though their yield is nominally less than that of the earlier larger devices, technical developments have rendered them increasingly lethal and accurate.

Over the years, three basic strategic or long-range nuclear-weapon delivery systems have been developed: (1) land-based intercontinental ballistic missiles (ICBMs) which may carry one or several independently targetable warheads (MIRVs, i.e., multiple independently targetable re-entry vehicles); (2) submarine-launched ballistic missiles (SLBMs); and (3) long-range bombers, which may carry gravity bombs and/or cruise missiles. While there is no clear borderline between strategic and the various shorter-range nuclear-weapons systems, it is common practice to regard such a system as strategic if it has a range above 6,400 kilometres (3,450 nautical miles); intermediate-range, between 2,400 and 6,400 kilometres (between 1,300 and 3,450 nautical miles); medium-range, between 800 and 2,400 kilometres (between 430 and 1,300 nautical miles); short-range, under 800 kilometres (430 nautical miles); and tactical if it is intended for use on the battlefield.

Modern weapons systems include a number of components: the warhead; the missile or vehicle that transports the warhead to the target; the platform — land-based launcher, bomber, or submarine — from which the vehicle is launched; and the command, control, communication and intelligence systems which exercise restraining or guiding power over the nuclear forces themselves. The single most outstanding feature in warhead development has been the reduction of size and weight in relation to yield, which has made possible the design of multiple warheads on ballistic missiles. An additional factor has been the increased sophistication of the guidance systems and the resulting accuracy of the delivery vehicle, which can currently release warheads within a few hundred metres of their assigned targets. Improvements in the delivery systems of nuclear weapons have had a great impact upon the nuclear arms race and would have been virtually impossible without the testing of nuclear weapons and delivery vehicles. Among other things, nuclear-weapon tests have been used to enhance yield-to-weight ratios and the so-called "tailoring" of weapons effects to specific military needs.

The dynamic of the nuclear arms race is to be found in the continuous drive to produce varied, accurate and effective nuclear-weapon systems. A step towards the further sophistication of nuclear arsenals on one side however has been followed by similar efforts on the other. Evidence of this pattern of action and counteraction goes back to the very beginning of the nuclear age.

In 1984, the world stockpile of nuclear weapons was estimated to be equivalent to some 15,000 megatons of TNT. This destructive capacity is considered to be 5,000 times greater than that used during the entire Second World War. The number of missile-deliverable strategic warheads of the two major Powers is estimated to have increased from about 3,700 in 1970 to some 16,000 in 1984, and there are also many more shorter-range and tactical nuclear weapons in various potential areas of conflict. Among the five nuclear-weapon States, the United States and the USSR possess by far the largest arsenals of nuclear weapons and the most advanced delivery systems.

The consequences of the possible use of nuclear weapons are such that they could not be confined to the nuclear adversaries but would threaten the rest of mankind. According to the 1984 World Health Organization (WHO) report, entitled *Effects of Nuclear War on Health and Health Services*, in an all-out nuclear war as many as 10,000 megatons of nuclear bombs could conceivably be exploded all over the world with 90 per cent in Europe, Asia and North America, and 10 per cent in Africa, Latin America and Oceania. As a result, half the world's population would instantly become victims of the war, with about 1.5 billion dead and 1.1 billion injured. In addition, millions of immediate survivors of an attack would die of radiation effects and disease over the next few years.

Recent studies and estimates suggest that climatic effects could also be produced by the use of nuclear weapons. According to some early estimates, such effects would include the blocking out of nearly all ordinary sunlight for several months due to smoke, dust and soot in the atmosphere. While estimated calculations reflect wide seasonal and geographic differences, a recent general calculation model assumed that an attack during the summer might decrease mean continental temperatures in the northern temperate zone by as much as 10°C to 25°C, (18°F to 45°F) with temperatures along the coast of the continents decreasing by a much smaller amount. According to some other calculations the temperatures would decline substantially, to some −23°C, roughly −10°F, and consequently, the survivors of a nuclear war would probably face freezing cold and famine in addition to the other known effects of the explosions.

Pursuant to specific requests of the General Assembly and with the assistance of governmental experts, two major reports on nuclear weapons have been prepared in the United Nations: *Effects of the Possible Use of Nuclear Weapons and the Security and Economic Implications for States of the Acquisition and Further Development of These Weapons (1968); Comprehensive Study on Nuclear Weapons (1980)*. The later one gives an analysis of existing nuclear arsenals and of technological developments in nuclear-weapons systems which occurred over the years. The study also discusses implications of doctrines of nuclear deterrence. In this connection, it suggests that a world system of nuclear-weapon States and non-nuclear-weapon States is unlikely to persist indefinitely, for such a system carries with it the seeds of nuclear-weapon proliferation. On the other hand, the study points out the existence of an inverse relationship between security and the qualitative and quantitative improvement of nuclear weapons, and concludes that even if the road to nuclear disarmament is a long and difficult one, there is no alternative to it. A system of international security based on the observance of the principles of the United Nations Charter and other universally accepted instruments of international law would eliminate the need for nuclear weapons and provide the basis for international security and peace.

Over the years, a very wide spectrum of measures has been proposed in the United Nations and other multilateral forums, covering limitations, reductions and the elimination of nuclear weapons and their delivery systems, including the cessation of production of nuclear weapons, the cut-off of the production of fissionable material for weapons purposes, and the restriction or prohibition of the deployment by nuclear-weapon States of nuclear weapons in the territories of other States.

There have also been negotiations in bilateral forums concerning nuclear weapons, and a number of agreements on that subject have been reached, in particular between the Soviet Union and the United States (see chapter I).

The pace of technological innovations and the resulting continuous improvement and sophistication in nuclear-weapon systems have been, however, much faster than the pace and achievements of disarmament efforts.

Cessation of the nuclear arms race and nuclear disarmament

Proposals for measures concerning the cessation of the nuclear arms race go back to the early period of disarmament efforts within the framework of the United Nations.

Especially since the mid-1960s, the importance of the question of nuclear disarmament has been increasingly recognized and voiced in all disarmament forums, as well as in many documents. Thus, paragraph 20 of the Final Document of the first special session of the General Assembly devoted to disarmament stated that, among the measures for the cessation of the arms race, effective measures of nuclear disarmament and the prevention of nuclear war have the highest priority. It further stressed, in paragraph 47, that nuclear weapons pose the greatest danger to mankind and to the survival of civilization and, in paragraph 50, that the achievement of nuclear disarmament will require urgent negotiation of agreements at appropriate stages and with adequate measures of verification satisfactory to the States concerned for: (a) cessation of the qualitative improvement and development of nuclear-weapons systems; (b) cessation of the production of all types of nuclear weapons and their means of delivery and of the production of fissionable material for weapons purposes; and (c) a comprehensive, phased programme with agreed time-frames, whenever feasible, for progressive and balanced reductions of stockpiles of nuclear weapons and their means of delivery, leading to their ultimate and complete elimination at the earliest possible time.

Since then, the General Assembly has repeatedly called upon the nuclear-weapon States, especially the Soviet Union and the United States, to initiate negotiations on the question of the cessation of the nuclear arms race and nuclear disarmament, in accordance with the provisions of paragraph 50 of the Final Document, and has adopted a number of resolutions on the subject.

In the light of the critical nature of the issue, the cessation of the nuclear arms race and nuclear disarmament received particular attention at the second special session of the General Assembly devoted to disarmament, in 1982. However, the views expressed by States during the debate were quite divergent and mainly reiterated their general positions on the nuclear arms race and nuclear disarmament.

The United States recognized that agreements on arms control and disarmament could reinforce peace and emphasized that new and bolder steps were needed to calm an uneasy world. It also stressed that such agreements must be equitable, militarily significant, verifiable and designed to stabilize forces at lower levels.

The USSR addressed the issue of the cessation of the nuclear arms race and nuclear disarmament from two angles. As discussed in the next section, it informed the Assembly of its unilateral undertaking not to be the first to use nuclear weapons. In addition, it stated that it supported the idea of a mutual nuclear freeze, also discussed later.

China, after reiterating its long-standing pledge not to be the first to use nuclear weapons, particularly emphasized that the United States and the Soviet Union should take the lead in stopping the testing, improvement and manufacture of nuclear weapons and should reduce by 50 per cent all types of their nuclear weapons and means of delivery. After that, China would be ready to join all other nuclear-weapon States in stopping the development and production of nuclear weapons and in reducing their respective nuclear arsenals according to an agreed scale and procedure, as a step towards their elimination.

The United Kingdom recognized that a better system of preventing war than nuclear deterrence must be sought, but held that it would be a perilous pretence to suggest that there was such a system within reach at that time. For the nuclear-weapon Powers, in its view, the task was to harness the existence of nuclear weapons to the service of peace — a task in which their duty was to show restraint and responsibility — while the role of the non-nuclear-weapon countries should be to recognize that proliferation of nuclear weapons could not be the way to a safer world.

According to France, what was needed on a priority basis was a gradual de-escalation of the nuclear arms race of the two major Powers. It further emphasized the importance of both eliminating destabilizing technology and reducing the imbalance of conventional forces, but maintained that what had guaranteed peace in Europe since 1945 was the certainty that any conflict on that continent would trigger a nuclear apocalypse.

Non-aligned countries generally saw an urgent need for multilateral negotiations on the cessation of the nuclear arms race and nuclear disarmament, leading to the adoption of concrete measures. In their opinion, all nations, whether or not possessing nuclear weapons, had a vital interest in nuclear disarmament measures, because nuclear weapons threatened the entire world. The members of the group stressed that an unrestrained nuclear arms race, instead of strengthening international security, on the contrary weakened it.

In 1983 and 1984, the General Assembly held wide-ranging debates on nuclear arms limitation and disarmament. The two major nuclear-weapon Powers, among others, set out in some detail their respective

35

general positions concerning the nuclear armament situation and nuclear disarmament.

The United States President, in his address to the 1984 session of the General Assembly, stated that, having repaired its strength, the United States was ready for constructive negotiations with the Soviet Union, and emphasized that there was no sane alternative to negotiations on arms control and other issues. In keeping with that position, the United States was ready to extend various non-nuclear negotiating efforts to include negotiations on a wide range of issues of concern to both sides, such as the relationship between defensive and offensive forces and what has been called the militarization of space. Expressing the hope for a historic breakthrough in arms control, he pointed out that agreement would depend upon the ability to control competition in offensive arms and achieve genuine stability at substantially lower levels of nuclear arms. In addition, he made concrete proposals for improving relations with the Soviet Union in order to reduce political suspicions and anxieties which were, in his view, the fundamental cause of the arms competition. He specifically proposed regular ministerial or cabinet-level meetings between the two countries, the exchanges of observers at military exercises and visits of experts to nuclear test sites.

The Soviet Foreign Minister, speaking on behalf of the President of the USSR, stated that according to the Soviet Union, a policy of realism, rather than of force, was necessary to solve the world's problems. In its view, if the United States showed such realism and accepted the principle of equality and equal security, then accords were possible. The Foreign Minister emphasized that since the United States was trying to achieve military superiority and to negotiate from a position of strength, anything aimed at reaching agreements on the basis of equality had been opposed by it. He reiterated the proposal for a freeze, both qualitative and quantitative, of nuclear weapons by all nuclear-weapon States, starting with the USSR and the United States, as a possible and necessary step to create confidence and a favourable atmosphere for a radical solution to the problem of nuclear arms. He put forward other proposals, including a pledge of non-first-use of nuclear weapons by all nuclear-weapon States and a pledge of non-use of military force between NATO and Warsaw Treaty countries.

The numerous resolutions dealing with nuclear questions adopted by the General Assembly at its sessions in 1983 and 1984 included several in which the Assembly reaffirmed the special responsibilities of the nuclear-weapon States for nuclear disarmament and for undertaking measures to prevent nuclear war and to halt the nuclear arms race in all its aspects, and in which it acknowledged the vital interests of all the people of the world in the success of disarmament negotiations. Basically, all resolutions dealing with substantive aspects of nuclear disarmament were adopted by majority votes, reflecting the long held positions of various geographical and political groups on this issue.

The question of the cessation of the nuclear arms race and nuclear disarmament has also been considered by the Disarmament Commission primarily in the context of the agenda item related to the nuclear arms race and nuclear disarmament. However, due to differences of view among the States members of the Disarmament Commission on the causes of the nuclear arms race, on the means to halt it and to prevent nuclear war, as well as on measures to reach nuclear disarmament, the Commission had not been able to reach consensus on a set of recommendations concerning these issues, as of the end of 1984. The Commission has also discussed the question in connection with the Declaration of the 1980s as the Second Disarmament Decade.

In addition the matter has been dealt with in the Conference on Disarmament in Geneva. Owing to the differences of approach mentioned above, the Conference has been unable to establish an *ad hoc* committee to initiate multilateral negotiations for agreements on the cessation of the nuclear arms race and nuclear disarmament, as proposed by members of the group of 21 and by socialist States. In that connection, Western States have continued to hold the view that it is preferable, in the existing circumstances, to have substantive discussions on those issues in informal meetings of the Conference. As a result, the question of the cessation of the nuclear arms race and nuclear disarmament has been addressed at plenary meetings.

On the whole, Western States have taken the view that nuclear disarmament should occur as a part of a general process of disarmament involving the reduction of nuclear and conventional armaments and armed forces concurrently. They believe that the first aim of maintaining a military capability, including a nuclear capability, is to prevent war of any kind by demonstrating the ability to defend oneself against any level of potential threat. Thus, they consider that deterrence has served and continues to serve as an essential component in maintaining overall equilibrium between the forces of the two major military alliances and has thereby contributed to strategic stability. Further, they emphasize that their military doctrines are solely defensive and based on a commitment never to use force — whatever the weapon — other than in legitimate self-defence, in accordance with the Charter of the United Nations. Briefly, it is their belief that the elements of deterrence and defence, together with arms control and disarmament, are integral to the maintenance of peace and security. They consider that the single most significant way of enhancing security and stability in international relations is for all nations to live up to their obligations under the Charter of the United Nations.

France, in particular, has maintained that its nuclear potential is limited to the minimum level strictly necessary to guarantee its security and independence. It has taken the position that when the arsenals of the two major nuclear-weapon States are reduced to verified levels in such a way that it can be considered that the gap between potentials has changed in kind, and when significant progress has been made in the real reduction of conventional imbalances and towards the elimination of the chemical weapons threat, it will then be ready to join in efforts aimed at the limitation and reduction of nuclear arsenals.

A group of socialist States, for its part, drawing attention to its own proposals for entering into negotiations on ending the production of nuclear weapons and destroying them and also for holding consultations preparatory to such negotiations, has repeatedly stressed that no task is more important than the prevention of nuclear war. It is the belief of those States that cessation of the production, reduction and elimination of nuclear weapons should be implemented on a stage-by-stage, mutually acceptable and agreed basis. The degree of participation by nuclear-weapon States in the various measures under each stage should be determined with due regard for the quantitative and qualitative significance of their existing arsenals and those of other States concerned. The approximate balance in nuclear weapons should, in their view, be maintained at all stages during the gradual lowering of the levels of arsenals, and the security of all States should remain undiminished. The measures for the limitation of the nuclear arms race and for nuclear disarmament should be linked to the strengthening of the political and legal guarantees of the security of States. As one such measure, they propose that there should be no deployment of nuclear weapons on the territories of States where there are no such weapons at present. They express their continued readiness to begin negotiations on the whole spectrum of issues concerning nuclear disarmament.

China has reaffirmed its position in favour of the complete prohibition and total destruction of nuclear weapons. In this connection it has also reiterated its proposal that the United States and the Soviet Union should take the lead in adopting concrete measures after which China would be ready to join all other nuclear States in undertaking to stop the development and production of its nuclear weapons.

The group of 21 in the Conference has repeatedly referred to the provisions of the Final Document of the first special session of the General Assembly devoted to disarmament, which accord urgency to curbing the nuclear arms race and achieving nuclear disarmament. The group has reaffirmed its position that all nations have a vital interest in negotiations on nuclear disarmament, because the existence of nuclear weapons jeopardizes the security of both nuclear and non-nuclear-weapon States. In its view the competitive accumulation of nuclear arms by the nuclear-weapon States cannot be condoned on grounds that it is indispensable for their own security. In addition, the group has reiterated that military doctrines based on the possession of nuclear weapons are unacceptable because they make the future of mankind hostage to the perceived security requirements of the nuclear-weapon States.

As of the end of 1984, no tangible results had been achieved by the

Conference on Disarmament in these matters and its work on them may be expected to continue.

Non-use of nuclear weapons and prevention of nuclear war

Article 2, paragraph 4, of the Charter of the United Nations calls on all Members to refrain in their international relations from the threat or use of force against the territorial integrity or political independence of any State, or in any other manner inconsistent with the purposes of the United Nations. The United Nations has been particularly concerned about the possible use of nuclear weapons and has sought preventive measures against that threat. Proposals discussed at different times and in different contexts have ranged from unconditional prohibition of the use of nuclear weapons to prohibition of first use and conditional bans.

Over the years the General Assembly has passed a great number of resolutions dealing with various aspects of the non-use of nuclear weapons and prevention of nuclear war. With the exception of procedural resolutions, all resolutions have been adopted by vote. The voting has reflected deeply-rooted divergencies in approach, particularly among the nuclear-weapon States, which are based on their different strategic doctrines and national security perceptions. In 1961 the General Assembly adopted its first resolution on the prohibition of the use of nuclear weapons by a vote of 55 to 20, with 26 abstentions, by which it declared that the use of nuclear and thermonuclear weapons would be a direct violation of the Charter of the United Nations and that any State using such weapons would be considered as acting contrary to the laws of humanity and as committing a crime against mankind and civilization.

In 1967, at the request of the Soviet Union, the General Assembly placed on its agenda a separate item on the conclusion of a convention on banning the use of nuclear weapons. The request was accompanied by the text of a draft convention. The outcome of the Soviet initiative was the adoption of a resolution on that subject, by 77 votes to none, with 29 abstentions. By it, the Assembly, *inter alia*, expressed its conviction that it was essential to continue the examination of the question of the prohibition of the use of nuclear weapons and the conclusion of an appropriate international convention.

At the 1978 special session of the General Assembly devoted to disarmament, a new phase began in the continuing search for ways to eliminate the danger of nuclear war. The Final Document of that session declared: "Removing the threat of a world war—a nuclear war—is the most acute and urgent task of the present day" (paragraph 18). It emphasized that "the nuclear-weapon States have special responsibilities to undertake measures aimed at preventing the outbreak of nuclear war, and of the use of force in international relations, subject to the provisions of the Charter of the United Nations, including the use of nuclear weapons" (paragraph 57). Furthermore all States were called upon to "actively participate in efforts to bring about conditions in international relations among States in which a code of peaceful conduct of nations in international affairs could be agreed and which would preclude the use or threat of use of nuclear weapons" (paragraph 58).

During the special session, India submitted a draft resolution declaring that the use of nuclear weapons would be a violation of the Charter of the United Nations and a crime against humanity and should therefore be prohibited pending nuclear disarmament. The draft also requested all States to submit to the General Assembly proposals concerning the non-use of nuclear weapons and the avoidance of nuclear war in order that an international convention on the subject might be formulated through further discussion and agreement. As all decisions were meant to be taken by consensus, India did not press its draft to a vote. However, at the subsequent regular session of the General Assembly in 1978, the draft was submitted again, co-sponsored by 34 countries, mostly non-aligned, and adopted by a vote of 103 to 18 (United States and other Western countries), with 18 abstentions (USSR and other Eastern European countries), reflecting differing views on the issue by the various political and geographical groups. Between the first special session, in 1978, and the second special session, in 1982, each year at the initiative of India the General Assembly has adopted similar resolutions. The voting pattern has been much the same. Thus, the 1979 resolution (34/83 G) was adopted by a vote of 112 to 16, with 14 abstentions, the 1980 resolution (35/152 D) by 112 votes to 19, with 14 abstentions and the 1981 resolution (36/92 I) by 121 votes to 19, with 6 abstentions.

The United States and other Western countries casting negative votes on these resolutions have done so on the grounds *inter alia* that to outlaw the use of nuclear weapons under any circumstances would be inconsistent with the Charter, which provided that all States must not use or threaten to use force in their relations with other States except in self-defence or in other situations permitted under the Charter and did not outlaw nuclear means for deterrence or defence against attack. However, while deterrence was essential in the current unstable security climate, the United States did not view deterrence as an end in itself. According to it, dependence on dangerous weapons must be reduced, and a more stable balance must be sought at a much lower level of armaments.

In the view of the Soviet Union, the question of the prohibition of the use of nuclear weapons should be considered and decided upon in connection with the non-use of force in international relations and the strengthening of international legal guarantees of the security of States. In its opinion, the resolutions in question artificially divorced the issue of the prohibition of the use of nuclear weapons from the adoption of international political and legal measures to strengthen security for all States and from the problem of the non-use of force by States in international relations.

At its session in 1981, the General Assembly had before it, besides the draft initiated by India, two other draft resolutions concerning the question of the non-use of nuclear weapons and prevention of nuclear war. A draft submitted by the Soviet Union, entitled "Declaration on the prevention of nuclear catastrophe", stressed that there continued to be a dangerous growth of tension in the world and that the arms race was assuming unprecedented proportions. In its view, therefore, the United Nations would be taking firm and correct action if it issued a warning that there could never be any justification or pardon for statesmen taking a decision to be the first to use nuclear weapons and that any doctrine endorsing the first use of nuclear weapons would be incompatible with the principles of human morality and the ideals of the United Nations. The draft was adopted by a vote of 82 to 19, with 41 abstentions.

During the debate on the Declaration, a number of Western delegations noted inconsistencies between the Soviet draft and other statements of the USSR on the issue of the use of its nuclear weapons. The Federal Republic of Germany, in particular, stressed that to limit the ban on the use of force to the first use of certain weapons appeared to be implying that there might be other types of war which might be permissible. The United States emphasized that meaningful arms control would become prudently feasible only when Member States strictly adhered to Article 2, paragraph 4, of the Charter and thus refrained in their international relations from the threat or use of force against the territorial or political independence of any State.

The other draft resolution, initiated by Argentina, was adopted by consensus. It urged all nuclear-weapon States and other Member States that so desired to submit to the Secretary-General their views and suggestions on the prevention of nuclear war for consideration at the forthcoming special session on disarmament.

At the second special session of the General Assembly devoted to disarmament, in 1982, many delegations referred to the danger and likely effects of nuclear war and the consequent need to avoid the outbreak of a nuclear exchange. In his statement to the Assembly, the Secretary-General noted that, by its very nature, nuclear war could not remain limited and, once it began, there would be no way to contain it. The prevention of nuclear war was not only a moral imperative but also a question of survival, since, in addition to the human costs, the ecology of the world would be severely affected and the infrastructure of civilization would be shattered.

In the course of the session many speakers called for the early removal of the threat of nuclear war and put forward various suggestions and proposals. In a message read to the General Assembly, the President of the USSR declared that with immediate effect, the Soviet Union assumed an obligation not to be the first to use nuclear weapons. According to the message, the Soviet Union, in taking that decision had proceeded from the fact that, should a nuclear war start, it could mean the destruction of humankind and perhaps the end of life itself on earth.

In the Concluding Document of the second special session, the General Assembly reaffirmed the validity of the 1978 Final Document and expressed its profound preoccupation over the danger of war, in particular nuclear war, the prevention of which remained most acute and urgent, and called upon all Member States to consider as soon as possible relevant proposals designed to secure the avoidance of war, in particular nuclear war, thus ensuring that the survival of mankind was not endangered (paragraph 62).

Five draft resolutions, two of which dealt solely with the question of the non-use of nuclear weapons and the prevention of nuclear war, were presented at the special session, but the possibility of reaching a consensus did not materialize on that occasion and the sponsors, therefore, decided not to put them to a vote.

Three draft resolutions on the question were subsequently put to a vote at the regular session of the General Assembly in 1982. The draft entitled "Convention on the prohibition of the use of nuclear weapons", initiated by India and co-sponsored by several other non-aligned countries, requested the Committee on Disarmament to undertake on a priority basis negotiations with a view to achieving agreement on an international convention prohibiting the use or threat of use of nuclear weapons under any circumstances, taking as a basis the text of a draft convention annexed to the draft resolution. It was adopted by a vote of 117 to 17 (Western States), with 8 abstentions. The draft entitled "Prevention of nuclear war", also sponsored mainly by non-aligned States, requested the Committee on Disarmament to undertake negotiations with a view to achieving agreement on measures to prevent nuclear war. It was adopted by a vote of 130 to none, with 17 abstentions (Western States).

The draft entitled "Non-use of nuclear weapons and prevention of nuclear war", sponsored by Cuba, the German Democratic Republic, Romania and Viet Nam, stated that the solemn declarations by two nuclear-weapon States not to be the first to use nuclear weapons offered an important avenue to decrease the danger of nuclear war and expressed the hope that the other nuclear-weapon States would consider making similar declarations. It was adopted by a vote of 112 (including USSR) to 19 (including France, United Kingdom, United States and other Western countries) with 15 abstentions (including China).

At the beginning of 1983, after intensive negotiations, the CD agreed on the following reformulation of an item on its agenda entitled "Cessation of the nuclear arms race and nuclear disarmament; prevention of nuclear war, including all related matters". A number of working papers were submitted during the Committee's annual session. A paper of the group of 21 called for the setting up of an *ad hoc* working group to undertake negotiations on practical measures for the prevention of nuclear war. A group of socialist States also called for the establishment of an *ad hoc* working group to negotiate concrete steps on the question, including the renunciation by all nuclear-weapon States of the first use of nuclear weapons and the conclusion of a world-wide treaty on the non-use of force in international relations. The Federal Republic of Germany submitted a working paper that sought as its objective the prevention of all armed conflict, beginning with the prohibition of the threat or use of force, as stipulated in Article 2 of the Charter of the United Nations. However, there was no consensus on those proposals as well as on the proposal for the establishment of an *ad hoc* working group.

In 1984, for the first time, the Conference on Disarmament included in its agenda a separate item entitled "Prevention of nuclear war, including all related matters". The group of 21 again submitted a draft mandate for an *ad hoc* committee which would consider the relevant proposals and a group of socialist States submitted a working paper containing various suggestions on practical ways to prevent a nuclear war.

While all members recognized the importance of the prevention of nuclear war, there remained differences in approach between various groups. Socialist countries viewed the use of nuclear weapons as a crime against humanity and consistently condemned nuclear war as contrary to human conscience and reason and as a violation of the right to life. They reiterated the need for the establishment of an *ad hoc* committee to negotiate concrete steps, including the renunciation by all nuclear-weapon States of the first use of nuclear weapons and the conclusion of a world-wide treaty on the non-use of force in international relations.

The group of 21 considered the removal of the threat of nuclear war as the most acute and urgent task of the day. It therefore requested the Conference on Disarmament to undertake, as a matter of highest priority, negotiations on measures for the prevention of nuclear war and also called for the establishment of an *ad hoc* committee on the subject.

Western countries, however, believed that further discussion was necessary before negotiations could begin. Moreover, they maintained that it was insufficient to condemn only nuclear war. States should, in accordance with the Charter of the United Nations, condemn and ban all use of force, while taking steps to enhance confidence and stability. In that connection, they pointed out that members of NATO had repeatedly reaffirmed that none of their weapons, either nuclear or conventional, would ever be used except in response to armed attack.

As a result of the different approaches outlined above, matters related to the non-use of nuclear weapons and prevention of nuclear war were considered only in plenary meetings of the Conference.

In 1984, the General Assembly again had before it three draft resolutions on the question, which largely corresponded to resolutions adopted in previous years. The draft initiated by Argentina and co-sponsored by a number of other countries generally emphasized the utmost importance and urgency these countries attached to the issue of prevention of nuclear war. It noted that despite discussions on the question in the Conference on Disarmament for two years, the Conference had been unable to establish an appropriate subsidiary body to consider it. In addition, the resolution requested the Conference to undertake negotiations with a view to achieving agreement on appropriate and practical measures for the prevention of nuclear war and requested the Secretary-General to prepare a report on the subject matter, to be submitted to the General Assembly at its fortieth session, in 1985. The draft was adopted by a vote of 128 to 6, with 12 abstentions.

The draft resolution initiated by the German Democratic Republic and sponsored by a group of socialist countries pointed out the urgency for all nuclear-weapon States to renounce the first use of nuclear weapons and requested the Conference on Disarmament to consider the elaboration of an international instrument of a legally binding character laying down the obligation not to be the first to use nuclear weapons. The draft resolution was adopted by a vote of 101 to 19, with 17 abstentions.

The draft submitted by Australia, Canada, the Federal Republic of Germany, Italy, Japan and Norway was entitled "Prevention of nuclear war, including all related matters: prevention of war in the nuclear age". In the view of the sponsors, that formulation provided a more appropriate description of the overriding task of the international community. The draft reflected the general Western view that, while the prevention of nuclear war remained the most acute and urgent task of the day, the renunciation of force, restraint, concrete and verifiable results in arms control negotiations, and confidence-building measures must be considered concurrently if any solution was to be reached. Further, in their view, any effective strategy for the prevention of nuclear war must equally address the issue of conventional war. Cuba and Czechoslovakia, however, pointed out that the most urgent task was to prevent the outbreak of nuclear war. Argentina, India, Mexico and Yugoslavia submitted amendments so as to shift the emphasis of the draft resolution clearly to the nuclear aspects of the question. Thereupon, the sponsor requested that no action be taken on the draft and indicated that they were unable to support the other resolutions which, in their opinion, represented a rather narrow approach.

Nuclear-weapon freeze

The idea of freezing stockpiles of nuclear weapons at a given level as the first step in a comprehensive process of disarmament is not a new concept. As far back as 1962, this concept figured in draft treaties on general and complete disarmament put forward by the Soviet Union and the United States in the ENDC.

Two years later, in 1964, the United States submitted to the ENDC a specific plan for a verified freeze on the number and characteristics of offensive and defensive strategic nuclear delivery vehicles. The immediate objective of the proposal was to limit the quantities held by the East and the West to the existing levels and to prevent the development and deployment of vehicles of a significantly newer type. The Soviet Union at the time opposed the proposal, holding that it would in essence introduce control without disarmament and would allow the retention of all existing delivery means and the "overkill" capacity of the United States.

The non-aligned members of the ENDC, in seeking to reconcile differences in approach between the USSR and the United States, suggested that the idea of a freeze should be linked to other proposed collateral measures, such as non-proliferation and a cut-off in the production of fissionable material for weapons purposes.

In the course of the general debate in the General Assembly, in 1965, the United States reiterated that if progress were made on a freeze, it would be willing to explore the possibility of significant reductions in the number of delivery vehicles as well. Thus, in the ENDC in 1966, it again urged a freeze on offensive and defensive strategic bombers and missiles designed to carry nuclear weapons, to be followed by a reduction in the number of such delivery vehicles. At the same session, the Soviet Union urged, instead, the destruction, under appropriate international control, of all stockpiles of nuclear weapons and their delivery vehicles and a ban on the production of such weapons and vehicles. No specific proposals were put forward, however, with respect to such measures, and the question of a freeze evolved, in subsequent years, in the direction of limitation of nuclear weapons through proposals in strategic arms limitation talks (SALT) between the Soviet Union and the United States.

The matter again received considerable attention during the 1978 special session of the General Assembly. The Final Document, adopted by consensus, unanimously called for a halt and reversal of the nuclear arms race, which would include the cessation of the qualitative improvement and development of nuclear-weapon systems and the cessation of the production of all types of nuclear weapons and their means of delivery and the production of fissionable material for weapons purposes (paragraphs 47 and 50).

At the 1982 special session of the General Assembly the question of freezing the production of nuclear weapons at their existing level was the subject of two separate draft resolutions put forward by India, on the one hand, and by Mexico and Sweden, on the other. It was the first time that specific reference was made to a general freeze on nuclear weapons. Because of the absence of a consensus, however, the draft resolutions were carried over to the regular session of the General Assembly in 1982.

In resubmitting its proposal at the regular session in 1982, India emphasized the fact that nuclear weapons as weapons of mass destruction must be limited, reduced and eliminated wherever they existed. It was for that reason that the draft resolution called upon all nuclear-weapon States without exception to agree to a freeze on nuclear weapons and a simultaneous cut-off in the production of fissionable material for weapons purposes. The freeze must be followed immediately by negotiations on the reduction and subsequent elimination of all nuclear-weapon stockpiles, India stated.

In introducing the other draft resolution, Mexico observed that conditions were most propitious for a nuclear-weapon freeze since the United States and the Soviet Union were at the time equivalent in nuclear military power. The freeze would embrace (a) a comprehensive test ban; (b) the cessation of manufacture of nuclear weapons and their delivery vehicles; (c) a ban on all further deployment of such weapons; and (d) cessation of the production of fissionable material for weapons purposes. With regard to compliance, it stressed that the freeze would be subject to the verification procedures envisaged in the SALT I and SALT II agreements, as well as those agreed upon in the course of nuclear-test-ban negotiations, and argued that the monitoring procedures in use were widely regarded as providing adequate assurance of detection of a violation.

Western countries expressed a different assessment of the value of a freeze on nuclear weapons. The United States, in particular, did not believe that a freeze on the testing and deployment of new nuclear weapons and delivery systems would offer a sound basis for either major arms control reductions or a more stable balance in the strategic equation. According to the United States, a freeze would risk perpetuating and accentuating dangerous asymmetries in the strategic balance. Moreover, it would present difficult verification problems. The United States attached the greatest priority to achieving substantial reductions in arms, rather than a mere freeze at existing levels.

According to other Western countries, a freeze could be justified only if the participants fully enjoyed their right to security, that is, if there was a genuine balance at both the global and relevant sub-global levels. In the absence of such approximate parity, a freeze would amount to unilateral disarmament and certify the superiority of one side at an arbitrarily chosen moment. In their opinion, such a freeze could turn out to be a destabilizing, rather than a stabilizing, measure.

The Soviet Union, for its part, emphasized that the nuclear arms race must be halted once and for all. Therefore all the nuclear Powers must participate in a freeze. The USSR denied the contention that such a measure would be beneficial only to itself on the ground that it had nuclear superiority as in fact approximate parity existed, and such parity continued to exist in the area of both strategic and other nuclear weapons, as well as in the area of conventional forces. The Soviet Union stressed that parity would contribute to preserving peace and that, in order to reduce the level of arms, it must be at the lowest possible level.

Due to those differing positions among the various political and geographical groups, the two draft resolutions on the issues of a nuclear-weapon freeze were adopted by a vote of 122 to 16, with 6 abstentions and 119 to 17, with 5 abstentions, respectively.

In the course of 1983 and 1984, that issue was also considered in the Conference on Disarmament under the agenda item "Cessation of the nuclear arms race and nuclear disarmament".

The Soviet Union and other socialist countries, while believing that a freeze would be most efficient if undertaken by all the nuclear-weapon Powers simultaneously, suggested that it might be initiated by the Soviet Union and the United States, on the understanding that the other nuclear-weapon Powers would subsequently follow suit. Compliance with such a freeze, in their opinion, could be effectively verified by national technical means and, if necessary, additional measures could be worked out and agreed upon. The USSR stressed that it did not regard such a freeze as a goal in itself, but as an effective first step towards the reduction and, subsequently, the complete elimination of all nuclear weapons.

The United States and other Western countries reiterated their assessment of the value of a freeze on nuclear weapons, with the United States also noting that American and Western strategy was obliged to regard nuclear weapons as having as their single function the prevention of war and the preservation of peace. It did not believe, therefore, that a freeze on the testing and deployment of new nuclear weapons and delivery systems could provide the basis for substantial arms control reductions or for a more stable overall military balance.

The non-aligned, for their part, held that a nuclear-weapon freeze, while not an end in itself, would constitute an effective measure for creating a favourable environment for the conduct of negotiations on the limitation of nuclear arsenals.

India, in particular, pointed out to the Conference that the Political Declaration of the Seventh Conference of Heads of State or Government of Non-Aligned Countries, held at New Delhi in March 1983, had included a recommendation for a freeze on the development, production, stockpiling and deployment of nuclear weapons. A freeze on nuclear weapons was also called for in the New Delhi Declaration of 28 January 1985, issued by the heads of State or Government of Argentina, Greece, India, Mexico, Sweden and the United Republic of Tanzania, which was subsequently welcomed in the Conference on Disarmament by the group of 21.

Prohibition of the production of fissionable material for weapons purposes

Among other proposals for specific measures of nuclear disarmament, the cut-off of production of fissionable material for weapons purposes was at various stages, and particularly in the 1950s and 1960s, strongly advocated within disarmament negotiating bodies. For instance, the United States submitted several proposals for such a prohibition to the ENDC and the General Assembly during the 1960s. The measure figured prominently in lists of collateral measures that might be agreed upon by the ENDC outside the framework of general and complete disarmament. After the United States and the Soviet Union announced, in 1964, their unilateral decisions to reduce the production of fissile material for use in weapons, the United States declared that it was prepared to advance to a complete cut-off of production, with verification, and proposed that the nuclear Powers should agree to halt, prohibit and prevent all production of fissile material for use in weapons; to refrain from assisting any country in the production anywhere of such material; and to accept appropriate inspection.

The matter, though again touched upon on various occasions before 1978, came up anew at the first special session of the General Assembly devoted to disarmament. The Final Document of that session stated, *inter alia*, that the achievement of nuclear disarmament would require urgent negotiation of a number of agreements, among which the cessation of the production of fissionable material for weapons purposes was mentioned. In addition, among more specific initiatives and proposals at the session, Canada submitted one designed to arrest the momentum of the nuclear arms race by a "strategy of suffocation", consisting of a combination of four measures, including an agreement to prohibit all production of fissionable material for weapons purposes. Canada, in particular, considered that that strategy would be important for halting the nuclear arms race and for preventing the proliferation of nuclear weapons. It has, therefore, submitted a resolution to the General Assembly each year since that time, requesting the Committee on Disarmament, at an appropriate stage, in its work on the item entitled "Nuclear weapons in all aspects" to consider the question of adequately verified cessation and prohibition of the production of fissionable material for nuclear weapons and other nuclear explosive devices. The General Assembly has approved the resolution each year. In 1984, it was adopted by a vote of 140 to none, with 8 abstentions, and although the five nuclear Powers have usually abstained in the voting, for the first time, the USSR, together with other Eastern European States, supported the resolution.

Nuclear neutron weapons

The question of the prohibition of nuclear neutron weapons is a relatively new item on the agenda of the United Nations and related bodies. The interest in the subject-matter came as a result of breakthroughs in science and technology which allow the production of a weapon containing a small nuclear warhead designed to enhance radiation effects while minimizing the destructive blast and heat effects of a standard nuclear weapon.

A proposal for mutual renunciation of the production of neutron weapons was first put forward by the Soviet Union in late 1977. The following year, the Soviet Union and other Eastern European States submitted to the CCD a draft convention on the prohibition of the production, stockpiling, deployment and use of nuclear neutron weapons.

In opposing the concept of a convention on banning nuclear neutron weapons, the United States pointed out that the Soviet Union was focusing on a single aspect of the dangerous confrontation of nuclear and conventional forces deployed in Europe, instead of allowing the CCD to make serious efforts to develop arms control agreements that would contribute to international security. It also held that, since it was a nuclear weapon, the enhanced-radiation weapon should be dealt with within the context of the limitation of nuclear weapons and nuclear disarmament. Moreover, being a reduced-blast weapon, it would be basically defensive in nature.

Each year since 1981, the German Democratic Republic has introduced a resolution entitled "Prohibition of the nuclear neutron weapon", sponsored by various Eastern European and non-aligned countries. Those drafts, *inter alia*, have repeatedly requested the Committee on Disarmament to begin negotiations with a view to concluding a convention to prohibit the production, stockpiling, deployment and use of nuclear neutron weapons. In the view of the sponsors, a further postponement of such a prohibition might have serious consequences and would not be consistent with paragraph 50 of the Final Document, which makes the cessation of the qualitative improvement and development of nuclear-weapon systems the starting point of the process of nuclear disarmament.

All draft resolutions have been adopted by a vote which clearly reflects differing views on the subject-matter: 68-14-57 in 1981; 81-14-52 in 1982; 74-12-57 in 1983 and 71-11-53 in 1984. Western States have either voted against the resolution or abstained.

Bilateral negotiations

As already noted, a wide range of measures has been put forward, within or outside United Nations bodies, aiming at the cessation of the nuclear arms race and nuclear disarmament, including, in one form or another, limitations, reductions and/or the elimination of nuclear weapons and their delivery vehicles. Parallel to these multilateral efforts, the Soviet Union and the United States have considered such measures bilaterally, particularly measures on the limitation of strategic arms. In the process a number of important agreements have been reached.

The proposal to consider the question of strategic arms limitation as a separate issue was first put forward by the United States in January 1964, when it suggested in the ENDC that the two sides should explore a halt in the number and characteristics of their strategic nuclear offensive and defensive vehicles. The Soviet Union, in a subsequent exchange of communications with the United States, indicated a willingness to begin discussion. The agreement to this effect was announced on 1 July 1968 on the occasion of the opening for signature of the Treaty on the Non-Proliferation of Nuclear Weapons, but the actual negotiations started only in 1969.

STRATEGIC ARMS LIMITATION TALKS (SALT I)

The Strategic Arms Limitation Talks (SALT) between the Soviet Union and the United States were initiated in 1969. A "preliminary discussion of the questions involved" began in Helsinki in November 1969. The main negotiations opened in Vienna in April 1970. Sessions afterwards alternated between Helsinki and Vienna. After initial attempts to reach a comprehensive agreement did not materialize, on 20 May 1971 the Soviet Union and the United States announced that an understanding had been reached to concentrate on a permanent treaty to limit anti-ballistic missile systems, but at the same time to work out certain limitations on offensive systems and to combine negotiations for a more comprehensive and long-term agreement on the latter. An anti-ballistic missile (ABM) is a defensive weapon designed to destroy incoming ballistic missiles before they reach their targets.

At an early stage of the negotiations, in September 1971, two limited agreements were concluded: the Agreement on Measures to Reduce the Risk of Outbreak of Nuclear War and the Agreement on Measures to Improve the USA-USSR Direct Communication Link.

The first phase of the negotiations (SALT I) ended with the signing in Moscow on 26 May 1972 of two agreements: the Treaty on the Limitation of Anti-Ballistic Missile Systems (ABM Treaty) subsequently amended by a Protocol of 3 July 1974, and the Interim Agreement on Certain Measures with respect to the Limitation of Strategic Offensive Arms, with a Protocol attached. The Treaty, as required, was ratified by both sides.

By the ABM Treaty, the Soviet Union and the United States undertook not to develop, test or deploy mobile land-based or sea-based, air-based or space-based ABM systems. They also agreed to limit ABM systems to two sites with no more than 100 launchers at each site. In 1974, the Treaty was amended by a Protocol which limited each side to one ABM deployment area only. The Soviet Union chose to maintain its ABM system in the area centred on its capital, Moscow, and the United States chose to maintain its system in the ICBM deployment area in North Dakota. Subsequently, the United States decided not to deploy its ABM system at all.

The Interim Agreement on Certain Measures with respect to the Limitation of Strategic Offensive Arms was concluded for a period of five years. It was designed essentially as a holding measure, to provide time for further negotiations. The Agreement established quantitative limitations for the strategic offensive forces of the two sides, which undertook not to start construction of additional fixed land-based ballistic missile launchers and to limit submarine missile launchers and modern ballistic missile submarines to an agreed level for each side.

At the time of the signing of the Interim Agreement, the United States had 1,054 operational ICBM launchers, and the Soviet Union 1,618, of which some were still under construction. In addition to halting the overall number of fixed land-based ICBM launchers which each side could possess, the Agreement contained specific restrictions with regard to heavy ICBM launchers. Within those restrictions, modernization and replacement were permitted, but in the process of modernizing, the dimensions of silo launchers could not be significantly increased.

With regard to submarine missile launchers and modern ballistic missile submarines, the Agreement permitted the United States to reach, from its existing base level of 656 SLBM launchers on 41 ballistic missile submarines, a ceiling of 710 SLBM launchers on 44 submarines, and the Soviet Union, from its base level of 740 SLBM launchers on ballistic missile submarines, to reach a ceiling of 950 SLBM launchers on 62 modern ballistic missile submarines. The additional launchers, 54 for the United States and 210 for the Soviet Union, were permitted only as replacement for older ICBMs deployed prior to 1964 or SLBMs on older submarines.

The provisions concerning verification of compliance with the ABM Treaty and the Interim Agreement were identical. Specifically, each party would use its national technical means of verification and neither would interfere in the use of such means by the other. Deliberate concealment measures were prohibited. A Standing Consultative Commission was established (by a Memorandum of Understanding of December 1972) in order to discuss questions relating to each side's compliance with the SALT I agreements. The first such review was conducted at the Commission's special session in the fall of 1977. On that occasion, both sides

51

agreed that the Treaty had operated effectively during its first 5 years, that it had continued to serve national security interests and that it did not need to be amended at that time.

STRATEGIC ARMS LIMITATION TALKS (SALT II)

In accordance with article VII of the Interim Agreement by which the USSR and the United States undertook "to continue active negotiations for limitations on strategic offensive arms", the SALT II negotiations began in November 1972 in Geneva. The primary goal of those talks was to replace the Interim Agreement with a long-term comprehensive treaty providing broad and more detailed limits on all strategic offensive weapon systems.

At the Washington summit meeting in June 1973, the Agreement on Basic Principles of Negotiations on the Further Limitation of Strategic Offensive Arms was signed, by which the two sides agreed that the limitations placed on strategic offensive weapons would apply to both quantitative aspects and qualitative improvements, and also that the limitations must be subject to adequate verification by national technical means. The second understanding, of July 1974, signed in Moscow, reflected the decision of the two Governments to seek an agreement covering the period up to 1985, rather than a permanent one as envisaged in the 1973 Agreement on Basic Principles. A joint statement of 24 November 1974, issued after the Vladivostok summit meeting, further specified the provisions upon which the negotiations and subsequent agreement would be based. According to that statement, the new agreement would include the following limitations: (a) both sides would be entitled to have a certain agreed aggregate number of strategic delivery vehicles (ICBMs, SLBMs and heavy bombers); and (b) both sides would be entitled to have a certain agreed aggregate number of ICBMs and SLBMs equipped with MIRVs.

Subsequently, the United States announced that the "aggregate number" referred to in the statement would place a ceiling of 2,400 on strategic delivery vehicles for each side, of which only 1,320 could be armed with MIRVs. The total number would be composed of a combination of land-based missile launchers, submarine missile launchers, intercontinental bombers and certain other categories of weapons that would have the characteristics of strategic weapons.

The SALT II agreement, which was signed at Vienna on 18 June 1979, consists of three basic parts: (a) the Treaty on the Limitation of Strategic Offensive Arms and the Protocol attached thereto; (b) Agreed Statements and Common Understandings associated with various provisions of the Treaty and the Protocol; and (c) the Joint Statement of Principles and Basic Guidelines for Subsequent Negotiations on the Limitation of Strategic Arms. While SALT II has not been ratified by the United

States, two successive Presidents (Carter and Reagan) have declared that they would do nothing to jeopardize the Treaty as long as the Soviet Union abided by it. The Soviet Government has made similar statements regarding its intentions.

The Treaty sets the initial aggregate number of strategic delivery systems at 2,400 for each side, to take effect six months after the Treaty has been ratified and entered into force. The number would be reduced to 2,250 by the end of 1981. Included in the totals are launchers of ICBMs, SLBMs, heavy bombers and air-to-surface ballistic missiles (ASBMs) with ranges of over 600 kilometres (324 nautical miles). Within the aggregate ceiling, the Treaty places a number of sublimits on specific types of nuclear systems. However, each party is free, within the overall total aggregate ceiling of 2,250 and bearing in mind the sublimits, to determine the actual composition of the aggregate.

In addition to these limitations, the number of warheads for each type of weapon is limited to no more than 10 for ICBMs and ASBMs and to no more than 14 for SLBMs.

A Protocol to the Treaty bans the deployment of mobile ICBMs, of ground- and sea-based cruise missiles with ranges above 600 kilometres and of air-to-surface ballistic missiles through 1981.

The two sides, for the first time, provided a complete picture of their strategic forces as of the date of signing the Treaty as follows:

	United States	USSR
Launchers of ICBMs	1 054	1 398
Fixed launchers of ICBMs	1 054	1 398
Launchers of ICBMs equipped with MIRVs	550	608
Launchers of SLBMs	656	950
Launchers of SLBMs equipped with MIRVs	496	144
Heavy bombers	573	156
Heavy bombers equipped for cruise missiles capable of ranges in excess of 600 kilometres	3	0
Heavy bombers equipped only for ASBM (air-to-surface ballistic missiles)	0	0
ASBMs	0	0
ASBMs equipped with MIRVs	0	0

The Treaty, which was to remain in force to the end of 1985, defines and identifies various specific weapons and includes numerous detailed limitations on testing, deployment, modernization and replacement, or conversion of particular weapon systems.

Both the SALT I accords and the SALT II Treaty have similar provisions concerning verification based on national technical means available to both sides (photo-reconnaissance and other types of satellites, monitoring of test signals). In particular, the provisions ban interference with national means of verification or concealment which impedes verification of compliance.

A special Standing Consultative Commission, set up by the two countries in 1972, also deals with any questions or doubts about compliance with the SALT II agreements.

The General Assembly, while noting that the SALT II agreement was finally signed, welcomed the agreement reached by the parties to continue to pursue negotiations, in accordance with the principle of equality and equal security, on measures for the further limitation and reduction in the number of strategic arms, as well as for their further qualitative limitation. Many United Nations Member States, in strongly commending the results of the bilateral efforts of the two major Powers, expressed the view that the importance of the SALT negotiations was such as to transcend the interests of the two parties involved in them; that the pace of negotiations should be accelerated; that the scope should be broadened to provide for substantial reductions and important qualitative limitations; and that the General Assembly should be kept informed by the two Powers of their progress in these areas.

FURTHER STRATEGIC ARMS TALKS

Although the SALT II Treaty has not been formally ratified, the bilateral negotiating process on strategic nuclear weapons has continued. The new United States Administration, which took office in January 1981 and which was quite critical of SALT II, proposed a new approach which it termed the Strategic Arms Reduction Talks (START). Although dissatisfied with the fact that the United States has not yet ratified SALT II, the Soviet Union agreed to start negotiations, referring to the new talks as negotiations on the limitation and reduction of strategic arms. The talks started in Geneva in June 1982.

The initial United States START proposal called in general for:

— Reductions in deployed ballistic missile warheads by one third to 5,000 for each side, of which no more than 2,500 were to be on ICBMs;

— A limit of 850 deployed ballistic missiles;

— A cut in the total number of deployed ballistic missiles to about half the present United States level of 850;

— Equal levels of heavy bombers.

A Soviet response to the American START proposal provided in general for:

— Reductions in strategic nuclear delivery vehicles from the SALT II levels of 2,250 to 1,800 for each side;

— Reduction of warheads to an equal agreed level;

— A freeze on further deployment of United States forward-based systems within range of Soviet territory;

— Prohibition of all cruise missiles with a range in excess of 600 kilometres (324 nautical miles).

54

Among the reasons for the divergence in approach are differences in the geographical position and in the composition and characteristics of the strategic forces of the two sides.

When the fifth session of the negotiations ended on 8 December 1983, the Soviet Union stated that the deployment in Europe of new intermediate-range missiles by the United States, namely Pershing II and cruise missiles, was changing the global strategic situation and made it necessary for the Soviet Union "to review all problems under discussion at the START negotiations" and, as a result, no dates for the resumption of the negotiations could be fixed. The deployment, in accordance with a NATO decision of 12 December 1979, was viewed by the United States as necessary to offset Soviet deployments of SS-20s and the resulting asymmetries which, it held, had emerged in the nuclear balance.

Ever since the conclusion of the SALT I accords, the General Assembly has welcomed the bilateral efforts of the United States and the Soviet Union as an essential contribution to the process of arms limitation and disarmament. At the same time, the General Assembly has, in various resolutions adopted in this regard, although lately never unanimously, urged the two sides to expedite the reaching of agreement and to report to it on the progress of their negotiations. Recently, the Assembly, in expressing the view that nuclear disarmament is a universal concern of all States, suggested that negotiations on the subject should also take place in a subsidiary body of the Conference on Disarmament which could be limited to the parties concerned, namely, the Soviet Union and the United States, if this could facilitate such negotiations.

INTERMEDIATE/MEDIUM-RANGE NUCLEAR ARMS TALKS

The negotiations on intermediate/medium-range nuclear missiles are of relatively recent date and were prompted by the development and subsequent deployment in Europe of more and more modern types of this category of weapons. The issue received particular attention in the late 1970s.

Thus, at the NATO meeting in 1979, members of the organization stated that they noted that the Soviet Union had been reinforcing its long-range theatre nuclear forces (LRTNF) both qualitatively and quantitatively, most notably by the deployment of SS-20s, while Western LRTNF capabilities had remained static. In view of that, NATO countries decided to modernize their long-range theatre nuclear forces by the deployment in Europe (in 1983 at the earliest) of United States ground-launched systems comprising 108 Pershing II, which would replace existing Pershing I-A, and 464 cruise missiles. At the same time, the NATO countries pointed out that they regarded arms control as an integral part of the alliance's efforts to assure the undiminished security of its member States and to make the strategic situation between East and West more stable, more predictable and more manageable, at lower levels of armaments on both sides. For that reason, they expressed their willingness to negotiate limits on that deployment in exchange for reciprocal Soviet limitations, particularly on the new mobile SS-20 missile system. That decision came to be known as the "dual track decision". The Soviet Union, for its part, stated that the deployment of SS-20s was intended to replace older SS-4s and SS-5s and that rough parity existed between the two sides on this class of weapons.

The negotiations on intermediate/medium-range nuclear forces between the Soviet Union and the United States began in November 1981 in Geneva. The United States at first proposed the so-called zero option, whereby its planned deployment of modernized and new intermediate-range weapons would be cancelled, provided the USSR eliminated its missiles of the same category. The United States proposal called for the elimination of land-based intermediate-range missiles altogether. In the course of the negotiations, the Soviet Union maintained that there existed an approximate equality between Soviet and NATO nuclear forces in Europe and offered to reduce its SS-20s to the level of the nuclear forces of Great Britain and France, said to be 162. That would be feasible, however, only if NATO countries were to forgo planned new deployment entirely. The proposal was not acceptable to the United States for the reasons stated above, nor would the United Kingdom and France agree to consider their independent nuclear forces as an integral part of the NATO posture.

Again, in November 1983, the Soviet Union stated its willingness to reduce medium-range nuclear missiles in Europe to 140, without increasing their number in Asia if the United States were to forgo deployment. The United States rejected that offer and held that unless the Soviet Union were to accept the zero option, the latter would retain a monopoly on land-based intermediate-range nuclear forces in Europe. The Soviet Union, for its part, continued to object to the deployment of any new American nuclear missiles in Europe, maintaining that the zero option was basically inequitable as it did not take into account the United States forward-based systems and the British and French nuclear missiles.

Thus, the talks on intermediate/medium-range missiles became deadlocked with little possibility of any early agreement. In November 1983, after the arrival of the first components of Pershing II and cruise missiles in Europe, the Soviet Union discontinued the talks and announced that it would lift its unilateral moratorium on the further deployment of medium-range missiles. It also stated that, in agreement with the German Democratic Republic and Czechoslovakia, it would deploy nuclear missiles on their territories as well as other nuclear systems on the high seas aimed against targets in the United States.

As in the case of the negotiations on strategic nuclear arms, the United Nations, in various resolutions, expressed the hope for their successful outcome and, at the same time, called on the parties to report to the General Assembly on the progress of the talks and requested them to bear in mind the vital interests of all peoples of the world. In addition, the General Assembly urged the USSR and the United States to examine the possibility of merging the two series of negotiations (strategic and intermediate/medium-range) into a single forum and broadening their scope so as to embrace tactical or battlefield nuclear weapons as well.

In view of differences on the substantive issues involved between the negotiating parties, their respective allies and other Members of the United Nations, the resolutions could not be adopted by consensus.

NEW BILATERAL NEGOTIATIONS ON NUCLEAR AND SPACE ARMS

After a 13-month break in the Soviet-American talks on strategic and intermediate/medium-range nuclear weapons, Soviet Foreign Minister Andrei Gromyko and United States Secretary of State George Shultz met in January 1985 in Geneva to discuss without conditions the subject, objectives and framework of new negotiations. In a joint statement issued at the end of their meeting, they agreed to hold negotiations on nuclear and space arms. The subject of the negotiations would be a complex of questions concerning space and nuclear weapons, both strategic and intermediate/medium-range, with all those questions considered and resolved in their interrelationship. The objective of such talks would be to work out effective agreements aimed at preventing an arms race in space and terminating it on earth, at limiting and reducing nuclear arms and at strengthening strategic stability. The joint statement pointed out that "ultimately the forthcoming negotiations, just as efforts in general to limit and reduce arms, should lead to the complete elimination of nuclear arms everywhere."

The negotiations, which began in March 1985, are conducted by a delegation from each side that is divided into three groups to address, respectively, space arms (whether based on earth or in space), strategic nuclear weapons and intermediate/medium-range nuclear weapons.

Chapter V

Cessation of nuclear-weapon tests

It was in 1954 that suggestions were first made that an agreement to ban the testing of nuclear weapons could be considered on its own merits, either as an independent measure or as one item in an agreement on more comprehensive measures of disarmament. The hazardous radioactive fall-out from tests, particularly atmospheric, carried out in the early 1950s, caused mounting worry as the world learned of the spread of radioactive nuclides of strontium-90, caesium-137 and iodine-131 and of the mechanisms transferring these substances to body tissues through the food chain (for example, through milk from cows fed on grass contaminated by radioactive rain).

In that connection, in April 1954, in a letter to the Secretary-General of the United Nations, India's Prime Minister Jawaharlal Nehru called for a "standstill agreement" which would seek to end test explosions of nuclear weapons as a first step towards the discontinuance of the production and stockpiling of such weapons.

The following year, in 1955, the Soviet Union proposed a convention on the reduction of armaments and the prohibition of atomic weapons, which would include the discontinuance of tests of nuclear weapons. In 1956, the Soviet Union proposed that independently of any agreement on other disarmament issues, States should agree to partial measures, including the immediate discontinuance of thermonuclear-weapon testing.

Western countries, for their part, particularly the United States, the United Kingdom and France, in supporting the idea of the limitation and monitoring of nuclear tests in principle, maintained that this should be achieved only as a measure of a comprehensive programme of disarmament and with adequate measures of control.

As a compromise solution, Yugoslavia later that year urged an early implementation of initial disarmament measures which should include the cessation of nuclear tests with "such forms and degrees of control as are required". India also submitted a proposal on that issue.

Thus, by the end of 1956, the different approaches of States became clear: the Soviet Union and India were calling for an early and separate agreement on a ban of all nuclear tests without supervision, maintaining that no significant testing could go undetected; Yugoslavia urged such an agreement with control as might prove necessary; and the Western countries regarded the limitation and eventual ban of nuclear testing, with adequate supervision, as part of a comprehensive disarmament programme.

Starting in 1957, important developments regarding the positions of the nuclear Powers began to take place. The Soviet Union, in reiterating its proposal for an independent agreement on the "immediate cessation of all atomic and hydrogen tests if only for a period of two or three years", indicated its willingness to consider the establishment, on the basis of reciprocity, of control posts on its territory, in that of the United Kingdom, the United States and in the Pacific Ocean area for the purpose of verifying the agreement. The proposal was incorporated into a resolution adopted by the General Assembly that same year.

That initiative led to an exchange of letters between the Soviet Union and the United States in 1958, which resulted in an agreement between the two countries to convene a conference of experts to study the possibility of detecting violations of an eventual agreement on the suspension of nuclear tests. The resulting report considered it technically feasible to establish a workable and effective control system to detect violations of such an agreement. The control system itself would be under the direction of an international control organ.

As a result, the Soviet Union, the United Kingdom and the United States agreed to begin negotiations in Geneva. In fact, in 1958 the United Kingdom suspended nuclear tests after 23 September, the United States after 30 October and the Soviet Union after 3 November. That voluntary ban was maintained by the three Powers until September 1961, when the the USSR conducted the first resumed test, followed by the United States two weeks later.

France carried out its first nuclear-test explosion in 1960. It has consistently maintained that until there is agreement on nuclear disarmament — including an end to weapons production, reconversion of stocks and a ban on possession and use — its plans to conduct tests will go forward.

Partial test ban

The negotiations pursuant to the agreement began on 31 October 1958 as the Conference on the Discontinuance of Nuclear Weapon Tests, with the participation of the Soviet Union, the United Kingdom and the United States. A personal representative of the Secretary-General was also invited to attend.

At the outset of the negotiations, the Western Powers dropped their insistence that the discontinuance of nuclear testing should be dependent on progress in other fields of disarmament. There remained, however, differences of approach with the Soviet Union on the issue of detection of nuclear explosions in outer space and underground and there was substantial disagreement over the question of on-site inspection.

In the period from 1958 to the end of 1961, various meetings and exchanges of letters on a test ban took place between the three Powers. The complexity of the central problem led to successive deadlocks, interruptions and renewals of discussion and to shifts in position and searches for compromise and new approaches to verification.

In 1960, the Western Powers first and then the Soviet Union presented new proposals. Both of them called for a ban on all testing in the atmosphere, in outer space and under water, and underground above a seismic magnitude of 4.75. The Western Powers, however, proposed that 30 per cent of all unidentified seismic events below the threshold of 4.75 should be subject to on-site inspection. The Soviet Union maintained that the treaty should be associated with a moratorium on all testing below the threshold of 4.75, and with a system of control using national means of verification. After prolonged discussions the Western Powers agreed to the Soviet proposal, provided that a co-ordinated regional programme to improve detection procedures was instituted and that the moratorium on testing below the threshold was for a fixed term only. The position of the two sides appeared to be closer at this period than at any previous time.

In June 1961, the Soviet Union, however, in a further development, declared that the question of a test ban must be linked with general and complete disarmament. The Soviet Union kept this position until November, when it reiterated its proposal for a separate test ban without an international system of control, pending agreement on general and complete disarmament.

As a result of increased tensions in the overall relationship between the three Powers, the Conference adjourned in January 1962 *sine die*. Nevertheless, the momentum that had been built up on the issue of a nuclear-test ban did not quite dissipate. Two months later in Geneva, the ENDC established a sub-committee consisting of the Soviet Union, the United Kingdom and the United States in order to continue consideration of a treaty on a nuclear-test ban. The Sub-Committee had before it two 1961 proposals for a comprehensive agreement on cessation of tests: the United Kingdom-United States proposal of 18 April and the USSR proposal of 27 November.

In April 1962, eight non-aligned or neutral nations (Brazil, Burma, Ethiopia, India, Mexico, Nigeria, Sweden and United Arab Republic) presented a joint memorandum to the ENDC. The memorandum stated that there existed possibilities of establishing by agreement a system for continuous observation of seismic events on a purely scientific and non-political basis. The system could be based and built upon already existing national networks of observation posts and/or additional ones. An international commission would supervise the nature of events in doubt.

61

The United Kingdom and the United States submitted in August 1962 two alternative draft treaties. One was a comprehensive treaty envisaging a ban on tests in all environments and making provision for a quota of on-site inspections in the case of suspicious underground events. The other contemplated a test ban in the atmosphere, in outer space and under water, without international verification. The two Powers explained that the partial treaty was submitted as a first step, since the Soviet Union considered that compulsory on-site inspection in a comprehensive test-ban treaty was not necessary. They also made clear that they would accept an uncontrolled moratorium of underground tests in the interim only if the treaty were to provide for an international system of verification.

The Soviet Union objected to both proposals on the ground that they ran counter to the eight-Power memorandum and maintained the principle of obligatory on-site inspections, though it made known that it was not opposed to considering a partial treaty, if underground tests were voluntarily suspended for as long as the problem remained unsolved.

The negotiations remained deadlocked because of disagreement on the issue of on-site inspection of unidentified underground events.

As far as on-site inspection was concerned, disagreement existed over a number of issues, including the initial insistence of the USSR to have all substantive operations of the proposed control commission subject to veto; the size of the area to be inspected, the nationality and composition of inspection terms and the criteria for identifying events that required inspection.

In December 1962, in an attempt to break the impasse, the Soviet Union proposed the use of automatic seismic stations ("black boxes") in addition to existing manned national means of detection. According to the proposal, the sealed boxes containing the instruments would be periodically replaced and carried to and from the headquarters of the international commission by national personnel on national aircraft, but international personnel could participate in their delivery and removal.

At the beginning of 1963, discussions in the ENDC revealed that there was agreement on the following principles:

(a) Utilization of nationally manned and nationally controlled seismic stations for detection and identification of seismic events;

(b) Installation of automatic seismic stations in the territories of nuclear Powers and adjacent countries, as a check on the proper functioning of the nationally manned stations. Delivery and removal of equipment and records of these stations would be carried out with the participation of foreign personnel;

(c) An annual quota of on-site inspections as a means to determine the nature of suspicious events.

After further clarification of positions, it turned out that disagreement between the Soviet Union and the Western Powers was basically limited to the number of annual inspections and to the number of automatic seismic stations. While the Soviet Union was proposing 2 or 3 on-site inspections a year, the United States proposed 8 to 10 (later reduced to 7), as well as the establishment of 7 automatic seismic stations.

In June 1963, the Soviet Union, the United Kingdom and the United States announced that they had agreed to hold talks in Moscow on the cessation of nuclear tests. On 2 July 1963, the Soviet Union made it clear that the insistence of the United States and the United Kingdom on on-site inspections made an underground ban impossible; therefore, it was prepared to sign a limited treaty banning tests in non-controversial environments: the atmosphere, outer space and under water.

The Moscow negotiations began in mid-July with the specific objective of achieving agreement on a partial nuclear-test ban. The Treaty was signed in Moscow on 5 August 1963 by the foreign ministers of the three nuclear Powers, designated as the depositaries of the Treaty, in the presence of the Secretary-General of the United Nations. It was opened for signature to all other States on 8 August 1963.

The parties to the Treaty commit themselves in the preamble to seek to achieve the discontinuance of all test explosions of nuclear weapons for all time and to continue negotiations for that purpose in order to put an end to the contamination of the human environment by radioactive substances.

According to its basic provisions, each of the parties undertakes to prohibit, to prevent and not to carry out any nuclear-weapon-test explosion or any other nuclear explosion in the atmosphere; beyond its limits, including outer space; under water, including territorial water or high seas; or in any other environment if such explosion causes radioactive debris to be present outside the territorial limits of the State under whose jurisdiction or control the explosion is conducted. Furthermore, the parties undertake to refrain from causing, encouraging, or in any way participating in, the carrying out of any nuclear-weapon-test explosions or any other nuclear explosion anywhere, which would take place in any of the three environments or have the effects referred to above.

The partial test-ban Treaty, which entered into force on 10 October 1963, had been ratified by 111 countries as of 31 December 1984.

The Treaty was the first international agreement of world-wide scope reached in the field of nuclear arms limitation. At the time, it was hailed as an event of historic significance that would begin to curb the nuclear arms race. Indeed, it greatly contributed to reducing radioactive pollution and to lessening international tensions. It also helped to create a climate that facilitated negotiations for other agreements in the field of nuclear arms limitation, notably the Treaty on the Non-Proliferation of Nuclear Weapons.

Issues concerning a comprehensive test ban

After the tripartite Conference on the Discontinuance of Nuclear Weapon Tests ended in early 1962, the task of seeking agreement on a comprehensive test ban fell mainly on the multilateral negotiating body in Geneva, the ENDC. Each year from 1962 on, the Committee considered the question of a comprehensive nuclear-test ban and regularly reported to the General Assembly. In its 1963 report, following the conclusion of the partial test-ban Treaty, the Committee expressed its satisfaction with the conclusion of the Treaty and "with the aims proclaimed by the negotiating parties in the preamble of the Treaty".

In the period between the signing of the partial test-ban Treaty, in 1963, and the signing of the non-proliferation Treaty, in 1968, there was no significant modification by the nuclear-weapon States of their positions on an underground test ban. While the United States and the United Kingdom acknowledged that some progress had been made in the technique of detection and identification of seismic events, in their view it was not enough to eliminate the need for on-site inspections. They were prepared to discuss the possibility of accepting a smaller number of on-site inspections than previously proposed, but did not suggest any new number. The Soviet Union continued to insist that no on-site inspections were necessary and that national detection systems were adequate and, in effect, it withdrew a previous offer of two or three on-site inspections a year.

The USSR urged a ban on underground tests above a threshold of seismic magnitude 4.75, with a voluntary moratorium on tests below that threshold. The United States continued to reject an unverified moratorium in any form. Various attempts by the non-aligned countries to mediate between the two sides were of no avail.

China conducted its first nuclear-weapon test in October 1964, thereby becoming the fifth nuclear-weapon State. The event provided the occasion for many Members of the United Nations to express concern not only about the testing in the atmosphere by China and France, but also about the continued underground testing by the USSR, the United Kingdom and the United States. In 1965, Sweden formally proposed international co-operation in the detection of underground explosions by the exchange of seismic data (the "detection club"). The following year, it proposed a system of "verification by challenge" or "inspection by invitation", where a party to a comprehensive test ban suspected of violation could provide information and invite inspection either on its own initiative or on request. Failure to do so would entitle other parties to withdraw from the treaty.

These proposals met with no immediate response from the two major nuclear-weapon Powers, which continued to maintain their respective positions on verification. In 1971 and in subsequent years, however, the multilateral negotiating body — the CCD — gave increased attention to the question of international co-operation in the exchange of seismic data.

At a special meeting of the CCD held on the occasion of the tenth anniversary of the partial test-ban Treaty, in 1973, nearly all speakers underlined the importance of the Treaty and the need to complete it with an underground test ban. The Soviet Union, the United Kingdom and the United States, in particular, stressed the role that the Treaty had played in reducing world tensions, curbing nuclear-arms proliferation and promoting arms limitation measures. At the same time, several non-aligned members of the CCD, supported by a number of Western countries, expressed strong dissatisfaction that the commitment of parties to the Treaty to seek to achieve the discontinuance of all nuclear-weapon tests had not been fulfilled, and several of them specifically expressed concern that such a failure could undermine the viability of the non-proliferation Treaty.

On 3 July 1974, the USSR and the United States signed the Treaty on the Limitation of Underground Nuclear Weapon Tests, commonly referred to as the threshold test-ban Treaty. Under that Treaty, the two countries undertook not to carry out, beginning 31 March 1976, any underground nuclear-weapon test having a yield in excess of 150 kilotons and to conduct all permitted tests solely within specified testing areas. Each party would use the national technical means of verification at its disposal and was under obligation not to interfere with the means of verification of the other party. The parties also agreed to exchange information necessary to improve the assessments of the yields of explosions.

The Treaty did not enter into force by 31 March 1976, the agreed cut-off date, and has not entered into force as of March 1985. However, the parties have stated that they would observe the limitation during the pre-ratification period.

In addition to the limit placed on the size of underground tests, each party committed itself to restrict the number of tests to a "minimum". Nevertheless, testing activities have not diminished.

In the CCD, several members welcomed the threshold test-ban Treaty as a step towards a comprehensive test ban. On the other hand, many members pointed out that the 150-kiloton yield threshold was so high (more than 10 times the yield of the Hiroshima bomb) that the limitation would not contribute to the cessation of the nuclear arms race. Moreover, the threshold exceeded by many times the level of verification capability. It was generally admitted that detection and identification of nuclear explosions of a much lower yield were possible. Furthermore, it was pointed out that the very concept of a threshold test ban, which implied the continuation of testing, was not consistent with the objective of a comprehensive test ban.

The provisions of the threshold test-ban Treaty did not extend to underground nuclear explosions for peaceful purposes. To fill that gap, the two Powers decided to work out a separate agreement for underground explosions for peaceful purposes. On 28 May 1976, they signed the Treaty on Underground Nuclear Explosions for Peaceful Purposes, commonly referred to as the peaceful nuclear explosions Treaty. The Treaty regulates the explosions which may be carried out by the Soviet Union and the United States outside their nuclear-weapon test sites and which may, therefore, be presumed to be for peaceful purposes. To ensure that explosions announced as peaceful should not provide weapon-related benefits that were not obtainable from weapon testing limited by the threshold test-ban Treaty, the new Treaty established the same yield threshold for explosions for peaceful applications as had been imposed on weapon tests, namely, 150 kilotons. In a Protocol setting forth specific operational arrangements, the two parties committed themselves to provide detailed information on explosions for peaceful purposes conducted by them and even to allow designated personnel of the other party to come within the area of explosion for observation purposes. Those provisions are generally considered as representing a significant advance in the question of verification.

The parties agreed that the peaceful nuclear explosions Treaty could not be terminated as long as the threshold test-ban Treaty was in force, since the former was an essential complement to the latter. The peaceful nuclear explosions Treaty also has not entered into force as of March 1985.

In 1975, for the first time since 1962, one of the nuclear-weapon States, the USSR, proposed a draft treaty on the complete and general prohibition of nuclear-weapon tests. The draft treaty, which was submitted to the General Assembly, provided for the prohibition of unlimited duration of all nuclear-weapon tests in all environments. It further provided that all nuclear-weapon States must ratify the treaty before its entry into force. As regards verification, the relevant provisions of the treaty were to be based on "national technical means of control", that is, there would be no on-site inspection. They contained, however, undertakings of the parties to co-operate in an international exchange of seismic data and to consult and make inquiries, as well as a procedure for lodging complaints with the Security Council in the case of a suspected violation.

In 1977, the USSR submitted to the CCD its 1975 draft treaty, together with an amendment which had been submitted to the Assembly at its 1976 regular session and which provided for on-site inspections by invitation under certain conditions.

Subsequently, Sweden also introduced a draft treaty with possible transitional arrangements permitting the two major nuclear-weapon Powers to phase out their testing over a limited period of time. On verification, the draft envisaged the establishment of a consultative committee of parties to the treaty to clarify ambiguous events. The draft also provided for the withdrawal of any party if all nuclear-weapon Powers had not adhered to it within a specific period. Sweden urged that a working group be set up at an early date to negotiate a concrete agreement on the matter.

In 1976, the CCD established the *Ad Hoc* Group of Scientific Experts to Consider International Co-operative Measures to Detect and Identify Seismic Events. The Group held its first meeting in 1976 and is continuing its work. In 1978, the Group submitted a comprehensive report to the CCD, recommending the establishment of a global network of seismological stations and the carrying out of a practical exercise to test the proposed network. The CCD, after considering the report, decided that the *Ad Hoc* Group should continue its work and study the scientific and methodological principles of the possible experimental testing of a global network of seismological stations of the kind which might be established in the future for international exchange of data under a treaty prohibiting nuclear-weapon tests, as well as under a protocol dealing with tests for peaceful purposes, which would be an integral part of the treaty. In 1979, the *Ad Hoc* Group submitted a second report on the subject. There was also a third report in 1984, and on that basis it was decided that an experiment be conducted.

In the Final Document of the first special session of the General Assembly on disarmament, held in 1978, the Member States of the United Nations recognized that the cessation of nuclear-weapon testing would make an important contribution to the goal of ending the qualitative improvement of nuclear weapons and the development of new types of such weapons, and of preventing the proliferation of nuclear weapons.

China stated that it found those parts of the Final Document dealing with the complete prohibition of nuclear tests totally unacceptable. Likewise, France dissociated itself from the idea that the cessation of nuclear tests would make a significant contribution to the prevention of the production of new types of weapons and the proliferation of nuclear weapons. In its view, the two most heavily armed Powers had, as a result of numerous tests, accumulated sufficient data to make any qualitative improvements they might desire, without carrying out new tests.

Following consultations between the Soviet Union and the United States in June 1977, trilateral negotiations, with the participation of the United Kingdom, began in July of that year for the achievement of a comprehensive test ban. Several rounds of those talks took place, the latest of which came to an end in October 1980.

The trilateral negotiations were private, and official information in regard to them was based on the progress reports that were provided from time to time to the multilateral negotiating body in Geneva by the United Kingdom on behalf of the three negotiating parties.

On 30 July 1980, for the first time, the three negotiating Powers submitted a tripartite, and more detailed, report to the Committee on Disarmament, which stated that they had agreed that the treaty would require each party to prohibit, prevent and not carry out any nuclear-weapon test explosion at any place under its jurisdiction or control in any environment; and refrain from causing, encouraging or in any way participating in the carrying out of any nuclear-weapon test explosion anywhere. They had also agreed that the treaty would be accompanied by a protocol on nuclear explosions for peaceful purposes, which would be an integral part of it. In the protocol, the parties would establish a moratorium on nuclear explosions for peaceful purposes and, accordingly, would refrain from causing, encouraging, permitting or in any way participating in the carrying out of such explosions until arrangements for conducting them were worked out which would be consistent with the treaty being negotiated, the partial test-ban Treaty and the non-proliferation Treaty.

According to the report, the parties were considering formulations relating to the duration of the treaty. They envisaged that a conference would be held at an appropriate time to review its operation. Decisions at the conference would require a majority of the parties to the treaty, including all parties that were permanent members of the Security Council of the United Nations.

The negotiating parties had agreed that a variety of verification measures should be provided to enhance confidence that all parties to the treaty were in strict compliance with it. The parties would use national technical means of verification at their disposal in a manner consistent with generally recognized principles of international law to verify compliance, and each party would undertake not to interfere with such means of verification. Furthermore, the negotiating parties had agreed to provisions establishing an international exchange of seismic data. Each party would have the right to participate in that exchange, to contribute data from designated seismic stations on its territory and to receive all the seismic data made available through the international exchange. Seismic data would be transmitted through the Global Telecommunications System of the World Meteorological Organization or through other agreed communications channels. International seismic data centres would be established in agreed locations, taking into account the desirability of appropriate geographical distribution.

The negotiating parties had also agreed to other co-operative measures. In particular, there would be provision in the treaty for direct consultations and for the exchange of inquiries and responses among parties in order to resolve questions that might arise concerning treaty compliance. If a party had questions regarding an event on the territory of any other party, it might request an on-site inspection for the purpose of ascertaining whether or not the event was a nuclear explosion. The requesting party should state the reasons for the request, including appropriate evidence. The party which received the request, understanding the importance of ensuring confidence among parties that treaty obligations were being fulfilled, should state whether or not it was prepared to agree to an inspection. If the party which received the request was not prepared to agree to an inspection on its territory, it should provide the reasons for its decision.

The three negotiating parties reported that they believed that the verification measures being negotiated broke significant new ground in international arms limitation efforts and would give all treaty parties the opportunity to participate in a substantial and constructive way in the process of verifying compliance with the treaty.

The three negotiating parties concluded their report by noting that they had gone far in their pursuit of a sound treaty and continued to believe that their trilateral negotiations offered the best approach. They were determined, they stated, to exert their best efforts and necessary will and persistence to bring the negotiations to an early and successful conclusion.

On 12 December 1980, the General Assembly adopted two resolutions on the cessation of nuclear-weapon tests. By resolution 35/145 A, initiated by non-aligned countries, the General Assembly reaffirmed the highest priority of a test-ban treaty, urged all States members of the Committee on Disarmament to support the creation of an *ad hoc* working group to start multilateral negotiations, and called upon the Soviet Union, the United Kingdom and the United States to halt tests without delay, either by a trilaterally agreed moratorium or unilaterally. The resolution was adopted by a vote to 111 to 2 (United Kingdom and United States), with 31 abstentions. By resolution 35/145 B, sponsored by Western countries, the Assembly called upon the three negotiating Powers to exert their best efforts to bring their negotiations to a successful conclusion and requested the Committee on Disarmament to take the necessary steps, including the establishment of a working group, to initiate multilateral substantive negotiations on a comprehensive test-ban treaty at its 1981 session. That resolution was adopted by a vote of 129 to none, with 16 abstentions.

At the 1981 sessions of the Committee on Disarmament, however, there was no consensus on the issue. In particular, the United States explained that the review of its policy concerning nuclear testing, including the question of negotiations on a test ban, had not yet been completed and in the circumstances it could not agree to the establishment of a working group. The United Kingdom held that the tripartite forum offered the most realistic approach. In 1981, the General Assembly again adopted two resolutions, 36/84 and 36/85, on the subject, which essentially renewed the requests contained in those of the previous year.

At the second special session of the General Assembly devoted to disarmament, in 1982, the great majority of States expressed deep concern not only at the lack of progress, but also at the apparent absence of any prospect of a breakthrough in a matter that was considered to be of the highest priority.

A few days after the conclusion of the second special session, on 20 July, the United States announced its decision not to resume the trilateral negotiations on a test-ban treaty. However, the Committee on Disarmament decided, in the course of its 1982 session, to establish an *ad hoc* working group "to discuss and define, through substantive examination, issues relating to verification and compliance with a view to making further progress towards a nuclear test ban". China and France made it known that they would not participate in the deliberations of the Working Group.

The establishment of the *Ad Hoc* Working Group fulfilled only in part the request of the General Assembly. Its mandate represented a compromise which took into account the concerns of the United States and other Western countries on the question. In the view of the United States, any consideration of a complete cessation of testing must be related to the ability of the Western nations to maintain credible deterrent forces and, while a test ban remained an element in the full-range of long-term United States arms control objectives, under the current circumstances, the United States held, a comprehensive test ban would not help reduce the threat of nuclear weapons or maintain the stability of the nuclear balance.

Additional resolutions were adopted by the General Assembly on the question in 1982 and 1983 (resolutions 37/72, 37/73, 37/85, 38/62, 38/63 and 38/72). By resolution 37/85 of 9 December 1982, the General Assembly referred to the Committee on Disarmament, for its consideration, the "Basic provisions of a treaty on the complete and general prohibition of nuclear-weapon tests", which was introduced by the Soviet Union and annexed to the resolution itself. The Assembly also called upon all the nuclear-weapon States, as a gesture of goodwill, not to conduct any nuclear explosions, starting from a date to be agreed upon among them and until the proposed treaty was concluded.

In 1983, although the item on a comprehensive nuclear-test ban was once again accorded the highest priority by the Committee on Disarmament, no substantive progress was made towards the achievement of that goal. A "Draft treaty banning any nuclear-weapon test explosion in any environment" was submitted, however, by Sweden on 14 June 1983. The draft, which was comprehensive in nature, provided for parties to keep under consideration the question of arrangements for peaceful purposes. Its verification arrangements, which would be ready for implementation when the treaty entered into force, included the international exchange of seismological and other data, as well as international on-site inspection and certain consultative, expert and secretariat machinery.

In 1984, the Conference on Disarmament renewed its consideration of a nuclear-test ban, particularly in connection with the question of the mandate for its *ad hoc* working body. A large number of delegations thought that the mandate of 1982 fell far short of the expectations of the international community. That mandate, in their view, did not correspond to repeated recommendations of the General Assembly for the urgent conclusion of a treaty on a nuclear-test ban. A new mandate should empower the subsidiary body to actually negotiate a treaty. While no delegation opposed the setting up of a subsidiary body, the Conference was not able to do so due to a deep divergence of views on the body's terms of reference.

The Assembly adopted three resolutions on a comprehensive test ban in 1984: 39/52, 39/53 and 39/60. They all reflected, in different language, the importance which the Member States of the United Nations attach to a nuclear test ban. Resolution 39/60, sponsored mainly by a group of socialist countries, urged the Conference on Disarmament to proceed promptly to negotiations with a view to elaborating a multilateral treaty. Resolution 39/52, tabled by non-aligned and neutral countries, also appealed to the members of the Conference to initiate immediately the multilateral negotiation of a treaty. Resolution 39/53, submitted by a number of Western States and other countries, while reaffirming the Assembly's conviction that a treaty was a matter of greatest importance, requested the Conference on Disarmament to resume immediately its substantive work relating to a comprehensive test ban, to take steps for the establishment of an international seismic monitoring network and to investigate other measures to monitor and verify compliance with such a ban.

On 12 December 1984, before the General Assembly took action on a number of disarmament items, including those on a comprehensive test ban, the Secretary-General of the United Nations, Mr. Javier Pérez de Cuéllar, made a statement in which, among other things, he appealed for a renewed effort towards a comprehensive test-ban treaty. He declared that a comprehensive test-ban treaty was a litmus test of the real willingness to pursue nuclear disarmament and continued: "Talks on a comprehensive test ban have been in abeyance for too long and their value has even been questioned. As with all arms-limitation negotiations, there will never be a perfect time to begin them in the opinion of all sides. The time to recommence these talks is now: they should not be delayed any further."

The conclusion of a comprehensive nuclear-test ban is of critical importance for the future of arms limitation and disarmament. As the 1980 report of the Secretary-General concluded, a comprehensive nuclear-test ban is regarded as the first and most urgent step towards the cessation of the nuclear arms race and, in particular, of its qualitative aspects. It could serve as an important measure for the non-proliferation of nuclear weapons, both vertical and horizontal. It would have a major arms limitation impact in that it would make it difficult, if not impossible, to develop new designs of nuclear weapons and would also place constraints on the modification of existing weapon designs.

The permanent cessation of all nuclear-weapon tests has long been sought by the world community and its achievement would be an event of great international significance.

Chapter VI

Non-proliferation of nuclear weapons

Negotiations leading to the Treaty

The concern of the international community that the newly discovered atomic energy should be used exclusively for peaceful purposes was voiced already in the very first resolution adopted by the United Nations General Assembly, in 1946. As knowledge of nuclear technology became more widespread in the 1950s, when a number of States began to render extensive technical assistance in the field of peaceful uses of atomic energy, this concern grew stronger and several proposals were put forward to prevent the spread of nuclear weapons.

The first proposals dealing directly with the spread of nuclear weapons were advanced by the Soviet Union and the United States in the Disarmament Commission in 1956 and 1957, respectively. The Soviet Union proposed a zone of limitation and inspection of armaments in Central Europe and a ban on both the stationing of atomic military formations and the deployment of atomic and hydrogen weapons of any kind in that zone. The Western Powers—Canada, France, the United Kingdom and the United States—presented a "package" of partial disarmament proposals, which included a commitment by each nuclear-weapon State party "not to transfer out of its control any nuclear weapons or to accept transfer to it of such weapons", except in cases where they would be used in self-defence against armed attack.

Thus different approaches developed with respect to the modalities of preventing the spread of nuclear weapons, namely, on the one hand, the creation of nuclear-weapon-free zones, and, on the other, the conclusion of a treaty which would specifically ban the dissemination of nuclear weapons by the nuclear Powers and the acquisition of nuclear weapons by States not possessing them.

The General Assembly's concern about the possible spread of nuclear weapons took concrete shape in 1958 and 1959, when Ireland submitted draft resolutions on the subject, suggesting in 1959 that the Ten-Nation Committee on Disarmament could consider appropriate means, including the possibility of an international agreement, whereby the nuclear-weapon States would refrain from handing over the control of such weapons to any nation not possessing them, and non-nuclear-weapon States would refrain from manufacturing any nuclear devices.

73

The Soviet Union, though concerned about the problem, did not support the resolution because, in its opinion, it would not deal with cases where nuclear weapons were transferred by a nuclear Power to the territory of an ally as long as the control of those weapons remained in the hands of the nuclear Power itself.

By another resolution initiated by Ireland in 1960, the Assembly called upon both the nuclear and the non-nuclear-weapon States, pending the negotiation and signing of permanent agreements, to declare at once their intention to refrain from all acts which would lead to the spread of nuclear weapons. The United States abstained in the vote on the ground that the resolution failed to recognize the central responsibility of the nuclear Powers to halt the stockpiling of nuclear weapons and its apparent call for an unverified commitment of indefinite duration.

In 1961, in an attempt to overcome disagreements existing between the nuclear Powers, Sweden submitted to the General Assembly a draft resolution proposing that the Secretary-General make an inquiry about the conditions under which countries not possessing nuclear weapons might be willing to enter into specific undertakings to refrain from manufacturing or otherwise acquiring them, and to refuse accepting them in the future on their territories on behalf of any other country.

The draft resolution was adopted and, accordingly, the Secretary-General requested Member States to express their views on the matter. Reciprocity was the condition for adherence to a non-proliferation treaty that was most frequently mentioned by the responding Governments. Some of them singled out specific States or all States within specified areas whose reciprocal adherence was required; others demanded universal adherence, also by non-Members of the United Nations. The three Western nuclear Powers indicated that the best solution would be general and complete disarmament under effective international control, which would include nuclear weapons. The USSR, on the other hand, supported the idea of nuclear-weapon-free zones, which, in its opinion, would contribute to building confidence between States and reduce the threat of an outbreak of military conflict.

Two draft proposals for treaties on general and complete disarmament introduced by the Soviet Union and the United States in the ENDC in 1962 contained provisions to prevent the dissemination or acquisition of nuclear weapons. Both countries also agreed to have the issue of non-proliferation discussed as a separate or collateral measure.

The problem of non-proliferation became a dominant issue in the discussion of the ENDC in 1965. A number of proposals and ideas were advanced by the non-aligned members of the Committee for the solution of the problem of non-proliferation. They generally held that a non-proliferation treaty should not be considered an end in itself; it should either become a part of a wider disarmament programme or be followed by an early halt in the production of nuclear weapons and a reduction in the existing stockpiles of the nuclear Powers. All the non-aligned members of the ENDC, however, declared their determination not to acquire nuclear weapons irrespective of their suggestions as to the form and scope of a non-proliferation treaty.

In August 1965, the United States submitted to the ENDC a draft treaty which would basically prohibit the nuclear Powers: (*a*) from transferring nuclear weapons to the national control of any non-nuclear State either directly or indirectly through a military alliance; and (*b*) from assisting any non-nuclear State in the manufacture of nuclear weapons. Under the draft, non-nuclear States would undertake corresponding obligations.

A month later, in September 1965, the Soviet Union submitted a draft treaty to the General Assembly which would prohibit the nuclear Powers from transferring nuclear weapons "directly or indirectly, through third States or groups of States not possessing nuclear weapons". It would also bar nuclear Powers from transferring "nuclear weapons, or control over them or their emplacement or use" to military units of non-nuclear allies, even if these were placed under joint command. Powers not possessing such weapons would undertake not to create, manufacture or prepare to manufacture them in any way.

Subsequent discussions centred mostly on the draft treaties presented by the USSR and the United States. Those countries themselves continued to hold conflicting views with respect to the question of nuclear defence arrangements within military alliances.

In order to facilitate the negotiating process, in March 1966 the United States introduced in the ENDC amendments to its draft treaty which sought to clarify and emphasize the Western view that collective defence arrangements would not violate the principle of non-proliferation. The United States also stressed that it would not relinquish its veto over the use of United States weapons. It reiterated, however, that it favoured the right of military allies to consult each other on the nuclear defence policy of the alliance. The USSR, for its part, stated that it was unwilling to sign a treaty which would not exclude all forms of participation by either the Federal Republic of Germany or other NATO non-nuclear Powers in the control of a nuclear deterrent of the Western alliance.

Despite strong disagreements on the issue of collective defence arrangements, it was apparent that both sides recognized the desirability of an agreement on non-proliferation. This concern was also shared by an increasing number of non-nuclear-weapon States, which in a series of resolutions in the General Assembly urged that non-proliferation receive priority attention.

In the fall of 1966, the United States and the USSR began private talks. A year later, they were able to submit separate but identical texts of a draft treaty to the ENDC. Following further suggestions from the non-nuclear-weapon States, a joint revised draft treaty was presented to the ENDC in March 1968. In the light of additional comments and proposals to strengthen the treaty, the United States and the Soviet Union submitted a new revised draft to the First Committee of the General Assembly in May 1968. The principal additional changes in the revised text concerned: (*a*) the availability of potential benefits of peaceful nuclear explosions to all parties (article V); (*b*) an undertaking to pursue negotiations in good faith on disarmament and to end the nuclear arms race (article VI); and (*c*) the right of groups of States to conclude agreements on nuclear-weapon-free zones (article VII).

In the ensuing debate, the USSR and the United States stressed that the prohibition already set forth in article I and article II effectively closed all possible loopholes for proliferation of nuclear weapons, directly or indirectly. Furthermore, by the terms of article III, non-nuclear-weapon States parties to the treaty were to negotiate with the International Atomic Energy Agency (IAEA) for the application of its safeguards system. Such a system would have the exclusive purpose of verifying the fulfilment of the treaty obligations, without affecting the economic and technological development of the non-nuclear States party to the Treaty or the possibility of international co-operation in the field of peaceful nuclear activities. The changes in article IV relating to peaceful uses of nuclear energy involved a modification in the language whereby the parties to the treaty would not only have the right to participate in the fullest possible exchange of equipment, materials and scientific and technological information for the peaceful uses of nuclear energy, but would also "undertake to facilitate" such an exchange.

On 12 June 1968, the General Assembly adopted a resolution commending the text and requesting the depositary Governments to open it for signature.

In the course of these extended negotiations, the concerns of the non-nuclear-weapon States focused particularly on three main issues: safeguards, a balance of mutual responsibilities and obligations and security assurances. As to the first issue, two problems were involved: the desire of the non-nuclear-weapon members of the European Atomic Energy Community (EURATOM), to preserve their regional system of safeguards and the widespread concern that IAEA safeguards might place non-nuclear-weapon States at a commercial and industrial disadvantage in developing nuclear energy for peaceful purposes, as nuclear-weapon States would not be required to accept safeguards. Subsequently, however, safeguards agreements were concluded between IAEA and the United Kingdom, the United States, France and the Soviet Union, which entered into force in 1979, 1980, 1981 and 1985, respectively. As to the balance of mutual responsibilities and obligations, most non-nuclear-weapon States held that their renunciation of nuclear weapons should not prevent them from using possible benefits of nuclear energy for peaceful purposes and that it should be accompanied by a commitment on the part of the nuclear-weapon States to reduce their nuclear arsenals and to make progress on measures of comprehensive disarmament. Articles IV and VI of the Treaty reflected that concern. As to security assurances, non-nuclear-weapon States sought guarantees that renunciation of nuclear arms would not place them at a permanent military disadvantage and make them vulnerable to nuclear threat. In this connection, the USSR, the United Kingdom and the United States agreed to provide certain assurances in a Security Council resolution.

Treaty on the Non-Proliferation of Nuclear Weapons

The Treaty was opened for signature on 1 July 1968 and was signed by three of the nuclear Powers: the USSR, the United Kingdom and the United States, and more than 50 other States. It entered into force on 5 March 1970 and by the end of 1984 it had been ratified by 125 countries.

France explained at the time that, while it would not sign the Treaty, it would behave in that field exactly as did the States adhering to it. China, while it has on various occasions expressed its critical views of the Treaty, has repeatedly stated that it does not advocate or encourage nuclear proliferation and that it does not help other States develop nuclear weapons. Although a considerable number of the non-nuclear-weapon States advanced in nuclear technology have ratified the Treaty, several others with a nuclear potential have not become parties to it.

On 18 May 1974, the Atomic Energy Commission of the Government of India announced that it had carried out a peaceful nuclear explosive experiment. On several subsequent occasions, India has reiterated its commitment to using nuclear energy for only peaceful purposes.

In the preamble of the Treaty, the States parties express their belief that "the proliferation of nuclear weapons would seriously enhance the danger of nuclear war". They also affirm the principle that the benefits of peaceful application of nuclear technology should be available to all parties to the Treaty and express their conviction "that, in furtherance of this principle, all Parties to the Treaty are entitled to participate in the fullest possible exchange of scientific information for, and to contribute alone or in co-operation with other States to, the further development of the applications of atomic energy for peaceful purposes". Furthermore, they declare "their intention to achieve at the earliest possible date the cessation of the nuclear arms race and to undertake effective measures in the direction of nuclear disarmament". In addition, they recall the determination expressed by the Parties to the 1963 Treaty banning nuclear weapon tests in the atmosphere, in outer space and under water in its Preamble to seek to achieve the discontinuance of all test explosions of nuclear weapons for all time and to continue negotiations to this end.

By the Treaty, each nuclear-weapon State party undertakes not to transfer to any recipient nuclear weapons or other nuclear explosive devices or control over them directly or indirectly, as well as not to assist, encourage or induce any non-nuclear-weapon State to manufacture or otherwise acquire such weapons or devices or control over such weapons or explosive devices (article I). On the other hand, each non-nuclear-weapon State party undertakes not to receive the transfer of nuclear weapons or other nuclear explosive devices or control over them directly or indirectly, and not to manufacture or otherwise acquire nuclear weapons or other nuclear explosive devices and not to seek or receive any assistance in the manufacture of nuclear weapons or other nuclear weapon devices (article II).

Non-nuclear-weapon States parties also undertake to accept safeguards, as set forth in an agreement to be negotiated and concluded with IAEA, for the purpose of verification of the fulfilment of the obligations assumed under the Treaty with a view to preventing diversion of nuclear energy from peaceful uses to nuclear weapons or other nuclear explosive devices (article III). By the end of 1984, 78 non-nuclear-weapon States had concluded safeguards agreements with IAEA in connection with the non-proliferation Treaty.

The parties also undertake to facilitate and have the right to participate in the fullest possible exchange of equipment, materials, and scientific and technological information for the peaceful uses of atomic energy. Potential benefits that might be developed by using nuclear explosions for peaceful purposes will be made available to non-nuclear-weapon States parties on a non-discriminatory basis and at the lowest possible cost. These States parties will be able to obtain such benefits pursuant to special international agreement(s) and through an appropriate international body or pursuant to bilateral agreements (articles IV and V).

In addition, the parties themselves undertake "to pursue negotiations in good faith on effective measures relating to the cessation of the nuclear arms race at an early date and to nuclear disarmament, and on a treaty on general and complete disarmament under strict and effective international control" (article VI).

Furthermore, nothing in the Treaty will affect the right of any group of States to conclude regional treaties in order to ensure the total absence of nuclear weapons in their respective territories (article VII).

The Treaty also contains provisions for amendments and envisages the procedure for the periodic review of its operation (article VIII). The Treaty is subject to ratification by signatory States and to accession to all other States. The Governments of the Soviet Union, the United Kingdom and the United States are designated the depositary Governments (article IX).

Finally, the Treaty provides that each party has the right to withdraw "if it decides that extraordinary events, related to the subject matter of this Treaty, have jeopardized the supreme interests of its country". It also states that a conference shall be convened 25 years after the entry into force of the Treaty "to decide whether the Treaty shall continue in force indefinitely, or shall be extended for an additional fixed period or periods".

Review Conferences

The Treaty provides, in article VIII, for a conference of its parties to be held in Geneva five years after its entry into force to review its operation with a view to ensuring that the purposes of the preamble and the provisions of the Treaty are being realized. It also provides that at intervals of five years thereafter review conferences may be held if a majority of the parties so wish. Accordingly, the First Review Conference of the Parties to the Treaty on the Non-Proliferation of Nuclear Weapons met in Geneva from 5 to 30 May 1975. The Conference adopted by consensus a Final Declaration, in which it reaffirmed the strong common interest of the parties in averting the future proliferation of nuclear weapons and reviewed the operation of the Treaty article by article.

At the First Review Conference much of the debate revolved around three matters that had already been discussed extensively in the course of negotiations leading to the conclusion of the Treaty, namely, nuclear disarmament, the security of the non-nuclear-weapon States against the use or threat of use of nuclear weapons, and the peaceful uses of atomic energy. The main difficulties at the Review Conference arose in connection with article VI of the Treaty, concerning the obligations of the nuclear-weapon State parties to pursue negotiations on nuclear disarmament.

The debate indicated that the gap in perceptions and expectations that had been discernible upon the Treaty's entry into force had not been bridged by the experiences of the first five years of its operation. The parties that tended to regard the Treaty as an arms limitation agreement primarily designed to constrain the further spread of nuclear weapons to countries not possessing them felt, on the whole, that the Treaty had fulfilled its purpose. By contrast, those countries that viewed the Treaty primarily as an effort to strike a balance between the mutual obligations and responsibilities of the nuclear and non-nuclear-weapon States felt that, in the implementation of the Treaty, the emphasis had been placed heavily on the obligations of the non-nuclear-weapon States, while scant attention had been paid to their rights or to the obligations of the nuclear-weapon States. Those different assessments were also reflected in the views expressed concerning the objectives of the Conference, the implementation of the provisions of the Treaty and the measures that should be taken to strengthen it.

On the one hand, the Soviet Union, the United Kingdom and the United States and most other Eastern and Western countries felt that the principal purpose of the Conference was to strengthen the Treaty by encouraging wider adherence to it and by taking measures towards a more effective safeguards system. On the other hand, the non-aligned and neutral States held that the main objective of the Conference was to make a thorough, critical examination of the Treaty's operation in order to determine whether all its provisions were being realized and to adopt measures required to fill gaps and remedy inadequacies that might become apparent during such an examination. Most of those countries believed that while it was vital to strengthen the Treaty to have States accede to it, that goal could be best achieved on the basis of an acceptable balance of the mutual responsibilities and obligations of the nuclear and non-nuclear-weapon States parties to the Treaty.

In the detailed discussion on the various provisions of the Treaty, all participants agreed that articles I and II had been faithfully observed by the parties. However, with respect to the provisions of the Treaty on the peaceful uses of nuclear energy and nuclear disarmament and on the related question of security guarantees to non-nuclear-weapon States, considerable dissatisfaction was expressed, which was reflected in various proposals submitted in the course of the Review Conference as well as in its Final Declaration.

The Second Review Conference, held in Geneva from 11 August to 7 September 1980, provided another opportunity for the parties to agree on ways to fulfil the various provisions of the Treaty and further strengthen the non-proliferation régime. Notwithstanding many positive developments, however, only a limited measure of agreement was achieved by the parties.

Virtually all speakers noted with satisfaction that the number of States parties to the Treaty had increased since the previous Review Conference. The United States pointed out that, together with France — which had made it clear that it would act as if it were a party to the Treaty — the countries that had adhered to the non-proliferation régime represented an aggregate population of over 2 billion people and an aggregate gross national product of 7.7 trillion, 98 per cent of the world's installed nuclear capacity and 95 per cent of its nuclear power reactors, and all major exporters of key nuclear materials and equipment. Several parties to the Treaty maintained, nevertheless, that the lack of universal adherence to the Treaty influenced negatively the process of its implementation. They also stressed that the nuclear capabilities of the countries which had not adhered to the Treaty were significant.

Of the various provisions of the non-proliferation Treaty, the most intense debate was on the implementation of article VI, concerning nuclear disarmament. Most participants held that the nuclear-weapon States had not adequately fulfilled their obligations to negotiate effective measures to halt the nuclear arms race and achieve nuclear disarmament. Accordingly, the major nuclear Powers were called upon to intensify their efforts in that direction. In reply, the three depositary Governments drew attention to the efforts they had made to reach agreement on a number of issues, including a comprehensive nuclear test ban, and to provide security guarantees to non-nuclear-weapon States.

The development and promotion of the peaceful uses of nuclear energy was also a major focus of attention in the general debate. A number of parties felt that it was necessary, however, to emphasize that the primary purpose of the Treaty had always been and remained the prevention of the spread of nuclear weapons. The participants generally expressed satisfaction with the IAEA safeguards procedures for existing facilities. However, they emphasized that those procedures would need continued improvement to deal with increasing amounts of nuclear material and increasingly complex nuclear fuel cycle facilities. It was recognized that, in order to cope with its growing tasks, IAEA would need adquate human and financial resources for research and development of safeguards techniques. The participants were agreed that non-nuclear-weapon States not parties to the Treaty should submit all their nuclear activities to IAEA safeguards, but there were fundamental differences over whether the suppliers were under an obligation to require such comprehensive safeguards of their customers.

A number of developing countries expressed dissatisfaction with what they considered to be restrictive export policies on the part of suppliers of nuclear equipment and technology for peaceful purposes towards developing countries parties to the non-proliferation Treaty. Regret was also expressed by some participants that suppliers which were parties to the Treaty had continued to engage in nuclear trade and co-operation with non-parties, often permitting less stringent safeguards than those applied to parties in accordance with the provisions of the Treaty. The view was also put forward that non-parties to the Treaty, including some relatively advanced countries, had benefitted more from the transfer of nuclear technology and equipment than needy countries which had adhered to the Treaty.

The question of security guarantees to non-nuclear-weapon States was also widely discussed. In general, there was broad support among the participants for stronger assurances to the non-nuclear-weapon States, and at the same time it was recognized that some progress had been achieved on the question of assurances since the First Review Conference.

By the end of the Conference, fundamental differences remained primarily on article VI of the Treaty, and because of those differences the Conference was unable to adopt an agreed final declaration. It simply recommended that a third conference to review the operation of the Treaty be convened in 1985.

Many participants expressed regret that the Conference had not been able, despite the agreement reached in a number of important areas, to produce by consensus a substantive final declaration on the operation and implementation of the Treaty since 1975 and on measures to be taken in the future. Nevertheless, delegations from all regions of the world affirmed their support for the Treaty and urged that work on the outstanding issues be continued.

In his closing statement, the President of the Review Conference, Mr. Ismat Kittani, sharing the disappointment of the Conference that it had not been able to reach a consensus on a substantive final document, said that the undertaking should be seen in all its complexity, which meant finding a common denominator among the positions of the States concerned on a matter influenced by both their individual views and the international climate. He noted that the prevention of the further spread of nuclear weapons had been the subject of very little controversy. While the question of the peaceful uses of nuclear energy had given rise to marked differences of opinion with regard to proposals on the relevant articles, it had been possible to obtain near unanimity in that area. The President noted that the differences at the Conference were mainly on the question of nuclear disarmament. It had to be admitted, the President stated, that the manner in which the obligations to pursue negotiations on measures for nuclear disarmament, contracted under the terms of article VI, were being honoured was disappointing. The arms race continued to intensify both qualitatively and quantitatively, and the prospects for a halt were far from bright. In that respect, he stressed that the warning given by a number of delegations was real and should be taken seriously.

After many months of preparation, the Third Review Conference will be held in Geneva for a period of up to four weeks, beginning on 27 August 1985, to assess once again how the purposes and provisions of the Treaty are being realized. Several complex and difficult issues will have to be addressed. Many non-nuclear States parties continue to feel strongly that article VI of the Treaty has not been adequately implemented. Yet the convergenge of the interests of the nuclear and non-nuclear-weapon States to check the further spread of nuclear weapons still exists. Indeed, many States have expressed the view that any further proliferation of nuclear weapons would make the attainment of nuclear disarmament a more remote goal and that it is therefore important to avoid the erosion of the Treaty's strength and credibility.

Security assurances to non-nuclear-weapon States

As discussed earlier, one of the central issues in the course of the negotiations of the non-proliferation Treaty was the question of adequate security assurances to non-nuclear-weapon States to counterbalance their undertaking to forgo the possession of nuclear weapons. After prolonged consideration of various options, the three nuclear-weapon States parties — the Soviet Union, the United Kingdom and the United States — agreed to provide such assurances through a United Nations Security Council resolution.

On 19 June 1968, the Security Council adopted resolution 255 (1968), by which it recognized that aggression with nuclear weapons, or the threat thereof, against a non-nuclear-weapon State party to the Treaty would call for immediate action by the Council and, above all, by its nuclear-weapon States permanent members. (China voted in favour of the resolution and France abstained.) The Council also welcomed the intention expressed by certain States to assist any non-nuclear-weapon State party to the non-proliferation Treaty that was a victim of an act or threat of nuclear aggression and reaffirmed the right to collective self-defence under Article 51 of the Charter of the United Nations.

However, a number of non-nuclear-weapon States, while welcoming the "positive" assurance provided for in the resolution, felt that it did not go far enough. They expressed preference for "negative" assurance, i.e., a commitment by nuclear-weapon States that they would not use nuclear weapons against non-nuclear-weapon States. Thus, the question of security assurances has continued to be actively considered at the United Nations and in other international forums.

This problem received particular attention in the course of the first special session of the General Assembly devoted to disarmament, in 1978. On that occasion, the five nuclear-weapon States made individual declarations designed to assure the non-nuclear-weapon States against the use or threat of use of nuclear weapons. China stated its readiness to undertake not to resort to the threat or use of nuclear weapons against non-nuclear countries and nuclear-weapon-free zones and reiterated that "at no time and in no circumstances will it be the first to use nuclear weapons". France stated that it was prepared to give assurances, in accordance with arrangements to be negotiated, to States that were part of nuclear-free zones. The Soviet Union said it "will never use nuclear weapons against those States which renounce the production and acquisition of such weapons and do not have them on their territories" and submitted a draft convention which would formalize such a commitment. The United Kingdom and the United States declared they would not use nuclear weapons against any non-nuclear-weapon State party to the non-proliferation Treaty or other binding commitment not to manufacture or acquire nuclear explosive devices, except in case of attack against them or their armed forces or their allies by such a State in association with a nuclear-weapon State.

Non-nuclear-weapon States, and in particular the non-aligned countries which have voluntarily remained outside the military alliances formed around the principal nuclear-weapon Powers, have repeatedly reiterated that, since they themselves have refrained from acquiring nuclear weapons, they are entitled to make demands with regard to the establishment of an adequate system of guarantees of their security.

For several years the General Assembly has at each of its regular sessions adopted two resolutions on security guarantees for non-nuclear-weapon States. One has been submitted each year by Pakistan. While noting the widespread support for an international convention, that resolution calls for the conclusion of effective international arrangements to assure non-nuclear States against the use or threat of use of nuclear weapons, taking into account any proposals on the question. The other has been submitted by the Soviet Union and, since 1979, by Bulgaria on behalf of other socialist States. It also takes note of the proposal that the nuclear-weapon States, as a first step, make identical undertakings not to use nuclear weapons against non-nuclear-weapon States having no such weapons on their territories. It also provides for the conclusion of an international convention on this issue.

The United States and other Western countries have supported a different approach, which is based on the premise that the many varying situations and concerns which must be taken into account by the five nuclear-weapon States probably preclude the conclusion of a common, generally acceptable international convention on security assurances. Accordingly, they have advocated individual statements by the five States, similar to those made at the first special session, and their embodiment in a single document.

The question has also been actively considered by the Conference on Disarmament. Each year, since 1979, it has established *ad hoc* working bodies on effective international arrangements to assure non-nuclear-weapon States against the use or threat of use of nuclear weapons.

The substantive discussion, which began in 1980, focused first on the scope and nature of such arrangements. While there has been general agreement that the objective should be adequate assurances to non-nuclear-weapon States, there have been divergent views as to scope and various criteria suggested for the application of mutually acceptable arrangements. Although there has been no objection in principle to the idea of an international convention, the difficulties involved have been clearly pointed out, particularly by Western States, which have accordingly suggested that a Security Council resolution might serve as a useful and effective international arrangement, while others, particularly the socialist members, consider that idea only as an interim measure.

In 1984, in its report to the General Assembly at its thirty-ninth session, the Conference on Disarmament reaffirmed that non-nuclear-weapon States should be effectively assured by the nuclear-weapon States against the use or threat of use of nuclear weapons, pending effective measures of nuclear disarmament. It noted, however, that differences related to the differing perceptions of security interests of some nuclear-weapon States and non-nuclear-weapon States persisted and that, under those circumstances, no progress had yet been achieved. The General Assembly, for its part, has, by two further resolutions, requested the Conference to continue to explore ways and means of overcoming the difficulties encountered in the negotiations in order to reach agreement on such effective international arrangements.

Peaceful uses of nuclear energy

Article IV of the non-proliferation Treaty is intended to assure non-nuclear-weapon States parties that they will not be prevented from benefitting from the use of nuclear technology and materials for the production of nuclear power and from other existing or future peaceful applications of nuclear energy.

Generally, both within the non-proliferation Treaty framework and outside it, the question of peaceful uses of nuclear energy has given rise to certain differences between countries which are suppliers of nuclear technology, equipment and materials and recipient countries whose economic development could benefit from the peaceful use of nuclear energy. The supplier countries have tended to place stress on precluding the possibility of the proliferation of nuclear weapons through peaceful endeavours, while recipients have placed stress on their right to develop peaceful nuclear programmes on the basis of non-discrimination and unrestricted technological exchange, in keeping with article IV of the Treaty.

The States which export various important nuclear items (such as nuclear reactors or material or facilities for the fabrication of fissionable material) have held consultations on the conditions they would set for such exports. One such condition is the demand that the exported item and the installation in which it is to be employed, as well as any nuclear material used or produced therein, be submitted to IAEA safeguards to ensure that neither the facility nor the material is used for any prohibited purpose. It is a requirement of the non-proliferation Treaty that the non-nuclear-weapon States parties accept such safeguards on all their nuclear facilities. The purpose of the safeguards system is to ensure the "timely detection" of the diversion of nuclear material to the manufacture of nuclear explosives or to unknown uses. Although the vast majority of installations are thus safeguarded, a number of States, some of which have considerable advanced nuclear technology, have not acceded to the Treaty and so are not obliged to accept such safeguards.

Questions related to the peaceful uses of nuclear energy have also been considered by the General Assembly. Two different approaches have developed through the years. Some countries, in particular Western and Eastern European countries, have emphasized the need for the application of so-called full-scope safeguards to the peaceful nuclear activities of non-nuclear-weapon States and have dwelt on the responsibilities of nuclear suppliers to ensure that the transfer of nuclear materials, equipment and technology does not contribute to the risk of nuclear-weapon proliferation. Developing countries, on the other hand, have generally laid stress on the significance of peaceful nuclear technology, equipment and materials for social and economic development. In that context, they maintain that international co-operation should be promoted with a view to permitting all countries to share equally in the benefits of the peaceful uses of nuclear energy, and consider that the restrictions applied by nuclear suppliers are unnecessarily rigid and, therefore, not conducive to stimulating such co-operation.

In order to facilitate the solution of some of these issues, the General Assembly in 1980 decided to convene the United Nations Conference for the Promotion of International Co-operation in the Peaceful Uses of Nuclear Energy and established a preparatory committee for that purpose.

The Preparatory Committee has held meetings every year since 1981. At the outset substantial differences emerged between the developed and the developing States about the purposes of the United Nations Conference and the way in which it should be conducted. In 1983, divergent views on such issues as a draft agenda, draft rules of procedure and the nature and form of the documents which should conclude its endeavours still persisted. As a result, the General Assembly decided that the Conference should be held in 1986, rather than in 1983, as originally planned, and urged all States to co-operate actively in its preparation. In 1984, the Committee reached agreement on most of the pending issues, including provisional rules of procedure for the Conference. In addition, the Committee decided that the Conference should be held at Geneva for a period of up to three weeks during the period September to November 1986.

International Atomic Energy Agency (IAEA)

The International Atomic Energy Agency (IAEA) entered the United Nations system in 1957 as an autonomous intergovernmental agency, having responsibility within the United Nations for international activities concerned with the peaceful uses of atomic energy. In March 1970, with the entry into force of the Treaty on the Non-Proliferation of Nuclear Weapons, the Agency was entrusted with the task of concluding, with the non-nuclear-weapon States parties to that Treaty, safeguards agreements covering all peaceful nuclear activities within their territories. Parties to the Treaty for the Prohibition of Nuclear Weapons in Latin America (Tlatelolco Treaty) have also concluded safeguards agreements with IAEA.

The safeguards system, which has been developed and expanded over the years to cover all types and sizes of nuclear plants, includes four main steps: (1) IAEA experts examine the design of a nation's existing nuclear plants and of new plants in the planning stage, in order to establish whether the design permits effective control. (2) The State is required to keep detailed records of plant operations and of the flow and inventory of nuclear materials. (3) The Government concerned supplies periodic reports to IAEA based on those records. (4) The Agency sends inspectors for on-site checks in nuclear plants. (Inspectors for each country are designated with the consent of that country.) The safeguards system constitutes the international community's first attempt to establish a system of control over an industry of strategic importance.

In June 1980, the Board of Governors of the Agency decided to establish the Committee on Assurances of Supply (CAS). That Committee, which is open to all member States of the Agency, has since advised IAEA on ways and means by which supplies of nuclear materials, equipment, technology and fuel cycle services may be ensured on a more predictable and long-term basis in accordance with mutually acceptable considerations of non-proliferation.

The Agency reports annually to the United Nations General Assembly and, as appropriate, to the Security Council and the Economic and Social Council. The General Conference of IAEA has responsibility over the policies and programmes of the Agency and is composed of all of its 112 member States, including the five nuclear-weapon States. Thirty-four countries are represented on the Board of Governors, which is the policy-making body of the Agency. IAEA is located in Vienna.

Chapter VII

Nuclear-weapon-free zones and zones of peace

Nuclear-weapon-free zones

The idea of establishing nuclear-weapon-free zones began to attract the attention of the international community in the 1950s as a means of limiting the areas where nuclear weapons could be deployed, tested or used. This concept was first introduced as a means to prevent or inhibit the further proliferation of nuclear weapons in specified geographical areas. The first formal proposal to this effect was made by Poland, whose Rapacki Plan of 1957 called for the permanent absence of nuclear weapons from the territories of several States in Central Europe.

Various proposals on the establishment of nuclear-weapon-free zones have been made since that time. The first concrete result was the Antarctic Treaty, concluded in 1959, applying a régime of denuclearization to an uninhabited area. Further results along that line were the Treaty on Principles Governing the Activities of States in the Exploration and Use of Outer Space, including the Moon and Other Celestial Bodies (the outer space Treaty), which was concluded in 1967, and the Treaty on the Prohibition of the Emplacement of Nuclear Weapons and Other Weapons of Mass Destruction on the Sea-Bed and the Ocean Floor and in the Subsoil Thereof (the sea-bed Treaty), concluded in 1971. A major milestone, however, was passed in 1967 when the States of the Latin American region concluded a treaty creating a nuclear-weapon-free zone in their continent, the first in a densely populated area, the Treaty for the Prohibition of Nuclear Weapons in Latin America (Treaty of Tlatelolco).

The concept of a nuclear-weapon-free zone was given new impetus in 1975, when a study on the question was carried out by an *ad hoc* group of governmental experts established by the CCD. The study entitled the *Comprehensive Study of the Question of Nuclear-Weapon-Free Zones in All its Aspects* stated, *inter alia*, that the development of interest in the concept of nuclear-weapon-free zones had been and continued to be due to the desire to secure the complete absence of nuclear weapons from various areas of the globe, where conditions were suitable. After examining the study, the General Assembly adopted a resolution, sponsored by seven non-aligned countries (Argentina, Mexico, Morocco, Nigeria, Pakistan, Peru and Zaire) by a vote of 82 (including China) to 10 (including France, United Kingdom and United States), with 36 abstentions (including Soviet Union), in which it defined the concept as follows:

"A nuclear-weapon-free zone shall, as a general rule, be deemed to be any zone recognized as such by the General Assembly of the United Nations, which any group of States, in the free exercise of their sovereignty, has established by virtue of a treaty or convention whereby: (a) The statute of total absence of nuclear weapons to which the zone shall be subject, including the procedure for the delimitation of the zone, is defined; (b) An international system of verification and control is established to guarantee compliance with the obligations deriving from that statute."

The resolution also set out the principal obligations of nuclear-weapon States towards such zones and the States they would include. It stated that in every case of a nuclear-weapon-free zone recognized as such by the Assembly, all nuclear-weapon States should undertake or reaffirm, in a solemn international instrument having full legally binding force, such as a treaty, a convention or a protocol, the following obligations:

(a) To respect in all its parts the statute of total absence of nuclear weapons defined in the treaty or convention serving as the constitutive instrument of the zone;

(b) To refrain from contributing in any way to the performance in the territories forming part of the zone of acts involving a violation of the treaty or convention;

(c) To refrain from using or threatening to use nuclear weapons against the States included in the zone.

The views expressed in the general debate underlined the divergence of positions on several issues in the study, in particular with regard to the definition of the zones and the obligations of nuclear-weapon States. The Soviet Union, for instance, indicated that it was not in a position automatically to give consent to obligations with regard to a nuclear-weapon-free zone contained in a treaty on the creation of a zone. The United States objected to the implications of the draft resolution, in particular with regard to the role and competence of the General Assembly. For the United States, the General Assembly could contribute to the establishment of a zone by providing a forum for consultations and encouraging States to work towards specific arrangements. The views expressed by the United States were supported by several Western countries which voted against the resolution. Other countries welcomed the study which, in their view, contained useful guidelines for the establishment of nuclear-weapon-free zones.

The 1978 Final Document of the first special session devoted to disarmament stated, in paragraphs 60 to 62, that the establishment of nuclear-weapon-free zones on the basis of arrangements freely arrived at among the States of the region concerned constituted an important disarmament measure. It also noted that the process of establishing such zones in different parts of the world should be encouraged with the ultimate objective of achieving a world entirely free of nuclear weapons. In the process of doing so, the characteristics of each region should be taken into account and States participating in such zones should undertake to comply fully with all the objectives, purposes and principles of the agreement or arrangements establishing the zones, thus ensuring that they were genuinely free from nuclear weapons. The Final Document also made clear that, with respect to such zones, the nuclear-weapon States in turn were called upon to give undertakings, in particular, to: (*a*) respect strictly the status of the nuclear-weapon-free zone and (*b*) refrain from the use or threat of use of nuclear weapons against the States of the zone.

In order to further specify and clarify issues related to nuclear-weapon-free zones, the General Assembly decided in 1982, at the initiative of Finland, that a new study should be undertaken to review and supplement the comprehensive study of 1975 and be completed by 1984.

Despite considerable efforts, the Group of Experts, appointed by the Secretary-General, was not able to reconcile differences in approach to various issues that emerged during the preparation of the study as a whole, and in particular with regard to its conclusions. The draft text of the study was then transmitted to the Secretary-General as it stood at the end of the final session in February 1985.

Treaties in force

International agreements to ensure the absence of nuclear weapons in certain areas and environments include the following: the Antarctic Treaty (1959); Treaty for the Prohibition of Nuclear Weapons in Latin America (1967); and the Treaty on the Prohibition of the Emplacement of Nuclear Weapons and Other Weapons of Mass Destruction on the Sea-Bed and the Ocean Floor and in the Subsoil Thereof (1971). In addition, nuclear weapons are excluded from outer space, the Moon and other celestial bodies (see chapter IX).

A. THE ANTARCTIC TREATY

The Antarctic Treaty, concluded on 1 December 1959, was the first international agreement which, by establishing a demilitarized zone, *ipso facto* ensured that nuclear weapons would not be introduced into a specified area.

The Treaty, which basically establishes that Antarctica is to be used for peaceful purposes only, was not intended to solve the problem of different territorial claims, but rather to ensure access to the whole of the area in order to carry out scientific research and to prevent it from becoming "the scene or object of international discord".

Article V of the Treaty specifically prohibits nuclear explosions and the disposal of radioactive waste material in Antarctica. It does not rule out those activities for peaceful purposes indefinitely but makes them subject to future international agreements on the question.

The prohibition against the introduction and testing of nuclear weapons falls within the scope of article I of the Treaty, which bans "any measures of a military nature" such as the establishment of military bases and fortifications, military manœuvres and the testing of any type of weapon. It does not, however, prevent the use of military personnel and equipment for scientific research and other peaceful purposes.

Under the Treaty's system of verification, observers appointed by each of the original contracting parties have the right of aerial observation and of complete access at all times to any area or installation.

The régime established by the Treaty has been scrupulously observed. This is reflected in the fact that no violations have been reported since it came into force and there has been no indication that any problems have arisen with regard to its verification.

The Treaty entered into force on 23 June 1961 and the number of parties to it has increased from the original 12 signatories in 1959 to 32 as of the end of 1984.

The question of Antarctica was raised anew in 1983 in the General Assembly. At the initiative of Malaysia, and with support from mostly non-aligned States, the Assembly adopted a resolution by which, *inter alia*, it requested the Secretary-General to prepare a comprehensive factual and objective study on all aspects of Antarctica, taking into account the Treaty as well as other relevant factors. The study, submitted to the 1984 session of the General Assembly, deals with the legal and political aspects, scientific research and natural resources in Antarctica, and also contains the views of 54 States on the issue. During the debate, Malaysia indicated that it would not at that time press its proposal for the establishment of a United Nations committee on Antarctica, but it insisted that any arrangements concerning that region's resources should be freely negotiated and concluded in a forum authorized or organized by the United Nations.

B.   TREATY FOR THE PROHIBITION OF NUCLEAR WEAPONS
IN LATIN AMERICA

The Treaty for the Prohibition of Nuclear Weapons in Latin America (Treaty of Tlatelolco) was the first Treaty to establish a nuclear-weapon-free zone in a densely populated area. It was also the first agreement to establish a system of international control and a permanent supervisory organ, the Agency for the Prohibition of Nuclear Weapons in Latin America (OPANAL).

Meeting in Mexico City in November 1964, 17 Latin American countries set up a preparatory commission to draw up a preliminary text for a denuclearization treaty, defining obligations and a system of control. After two years of negotiations, the Treaty was signed on 14 February 1967, at Tlatelolco, a borough of Mexico City, and was endorsed by the General Assembly later the same year.

The basic obligation of the parties to the Treaty, defined in article 1, is to use exclusively for peaceful purposes the nuclear material and facilities under their jurisdiction, and to prohibit and prevent in their respective territories the very presence of nuclear weapons for any purpose and under any circumstances.

Parties to the Treaty also undertake to refrain from engaging in, encouraging or authorizing, directly or indirectly, or in any way participating in the testing, use, manufacture, production, possession or control of any nuclear weapon.

OPANAL was set up in June 1969. Its control system includes safeguards to be negotiated with IAEA with respect to all the nuclear activities of the parties.

Annexed to the Treaty are two Additional Protocols which create a system of obligations for extra-continental and continental States having responsibility *de jure* or *de facto* for territories in the zone of application of the Treaty and for the nuclear-weapon States.

Thus, under Additional Protocol I, France, the Netherlands, the United Kingdom and the United States would agree to guarantee nuclear-weapon-free status to those territories for which they are, *de jure* or *de facto*, internationally responsible. The Protocol has been signed and ratified by the Netherlands, the United Kingdom and the United States. France has signed it and has declared that it will in due course take an appropriate decision.

Under Additional Protocol II, nuclear-weapon States pledge to respect fully the "denuclearization of Latin America in respect of warlike purposes" and "not to use or threaten to use nuclear weapons against the Contracting Parties". By 1979, all five nuclear-weapon States had adhered to it.

As of 31 December 1984, the Treaty was in force for 23 Latin American States that had ratified it and that had waived the requirements set out in article 28 (that all States in the zone be parties to the Treaty, that all States to which the Protocols apply adhere to them and that relevant safeguards agreements be concluded with IAEA).

C. SEA-BED TREATY

In the late 1960s, with marked advances in the science of oceanography and the growing interest of all nations in the potential resources available in the sea, the General Assembly became increasingly concerned with the need for an international régime to govern the uses of the sea-bed and ocean floor beyond territorial waters. In 1967, on the initiative of Malta, the Assembly discussed the question of reserving that area exclusively for peaceful purposes and exploiting its resources for the benefit of mankind. Special concern was expressed that it be done without impairment of the marine environment. The Assembly, therefore, established a sea-bed committee to deal with these matters.

The question of the regulation of the uses of the sea-bed was also discussed at length in the ENDC, from 1968 until the end of 1970. In a memorandum submitted in 1968, the Soviet Union proposed that there be an international agreement on limiting the military use of the sea-bed and ocean floor and, in particular, banning the establishment of fixed military installations. At the same time, the President of the United States, in a message to the ENDC, called on that body to begin negotiations on an agreement "which would prohibit the use of the new environment for the emplacement of weapons of mass destruction".

In 1969, the Soviet Union and the United States submitted a joint draft treaty to the ENDC. After intensive consideration in various bodies, a revised draft treaty was submitted to the General Assembly. The final draft was approved by a vote of 104 to 2 (El Salvador and Peru), with 2 abstentions (Ecuador and France), on 7 December 1970.

The Treaty provides that the States parties to it undertake not to place on or under the sea-bed, beyond the outer limit of a 12-mile coastal zone, any nuclear weapons or any other weapons of mass destruction or any facilities for such weapons. Each State party "shall have the right to verify through observation the activities of other States Parties" provided that "observation does not interfere with such activities". If one party doubts another's compliance with its obligations under the Treaty, the two parties are to hold consultations. If reasonable doubts persist, "the State Party having such doubts shall notify the other States Parties, and the Parties concerned shall co-operate on such further procedures for verification as may be agreed, including appropriate inspection of objects, structures, installations or other facilities". If consultation and co-operation do not remove the doubts concerning the fulfilment of the obligations assumed under the Treaty, a State party may, in accordance with the provisions of the United Nations Charter, refer the matter to the Security Council.

The Treaty was opened for signature on 11 February 1971. It entered into force on 18 May 1972. By the end of 1984, 74 States had become parties to the Treaty and another 28 had signed it.

Two Review Conferences of the Parties to the Treaty were held, in 1977 and 1983, to determine if the provisions of the Treaty were being realized (article VII). In the Final Declarations of both Review Conferences, the States parties confirmed that the obligations assumed under

94

article I of the Treaty had been faithfully observed. While making a favourable assessment of the effectiveness of the Treaty since 1972, they also recognized that it should be supplemented by additional measures to exclude the sea-bed area from the arms race. Accordingly, they suggested that the Conference on Disarmament consider the matter further, in consultation with the States parties to the Treaty. During its 1985 session, the Conference expressed the view, *inter alia*, that the scope of the sea-bed Treaty should be broadened, that its provisions governing procedures for verification and compliance should be improved and that access to information on relevant technological developments should be facilitated.

D. OUTER SPACE TREATY

The Treaty on Principles Governing the Activities of States in the Exploration and Use of Outer Space, including the Moon and Other Celestial Bodies was concluded in 1967 in order to ensure that that environment would be used for the benefit of all peoples. See chapter IX for a discussion of the Treaty.

Proposals for nuclear-weapon-free zones

Proposals for nuclear-weapon-free zones in several regions of the world have been discussed in the General Assembly and elsewhere for almost three decades. They have concerned such geographic areas as Africa, the Balkans, Central Europe, the Mediterranean, the Middle East, Northern Europe, South Africa and the South Pacific.

A. AFRICA

The interest of African countries in establishing a nuclear-weapon-free zone in their continent was first expressed in the early 1960s. Initially, their attention focused on obtaining agreement that the territory of Africa should not be used for nuclear test explosions and was related to the plans of France to carry out a series of test in the Sahara. In this connection, the General Assembly in 1961, acting on a proposal of 14 African States, called on Member States not to carry out nuclear tests in Africa in any form, to refrain from using Africa for storing or transporting nuclear weapons and to respect the continent as a nuclear-weapon-free zone. The resolution was adopted by a vote of 55 to none, with 44 abstentions.

Later on the concept was broadened. Thus, at a 1964 summit conference, the heads of State and Government of the Organization of African Unity (OAU) issued the Declaration on the Denuclearization of Africa, in which they solemnly declared their readiness to undertake, through an international agreement to be concluded under United Nations auspices, not to manufacture or control atomic weapons, and appealed to all peace-loving nations to accept the same undertaking and to all the nuclear Powers to respect the Declaration and conform to it.

Endorsing the Declaration in 1965, the General Assembly expressed the hope that African States would initiate studies to implement the denuclearization of the continent and take the necessary measures through OAU to achieve that end. It also requested the Secretary-General to extend to OAU any assistance requested for that purpose. At the same time, the Assembly called on all States not to transfer nuclear weapons, scientific data or technical assistance, either directly or indirectly, in any form that might be used to aid in the manufacture or use of nuclear weapons in Africa. The resolution was adopted by a vote of 105 to none, with 2 abstentions (France and Portugal).

Ten years after the Declaration of OAU, in 1974, the General Assembly adopted a resolution which called upon all States to consider and respect the continent of Africa as a nuclear-weapon-free zone, and every year since then, the General Assembly has adopted resolutions reiterating that appeal by the international community.

Meanwhile, grave concern has been expressed by the international community at South Africa's nuclear capability. The General Assembly, starting in 1976, in the context of its discussions on the establishment of a nuclear-weapon-free zone in Africa, has paid particular attention to developments related to activities of South Africa in the nuclear field and has adopted resolutions on the matter.

In 1979, as a result of a report indicating that a small nuclear explosion might have been conducted in the area of the Indian Ocean and the South Atlantic, the General Assembly on the initiative of Nigeria, requested the Secretary-General to undertake a study on South Africa's plan and its capability in the nuclear field.

The Study, prepared by the Group of Experts in 1981, stated, *inter alia*, that "there is no doubt that South Africa has the technical capability to make nuclear weapons and the necessary means of delivery" and expressed the view that the introduction of nuclear weapons into the African continent, and particularly in such a volatile region as southern Africa, would not only be a severe blow to world-wide efforts at non-proliferation, but would also upset many years' efforts to spare the African continent from the nuclear arms race and to make it a nuclear-weapon-free zone. The General Assembly, for its part, has adopted resolutions on the issue in all recent years. In 1983, it requested UNIDIR, in co-operation with the Department for Disarmament Affairs and in consultation with the OAU, to provide data on the continued development of South Africa's nuclear capability. The report was submitted to the Assembly in 1984.

The question of the nuclear capability of South Africa has been on the agenda of the Disarmament Commission since its re-establishment in 1979, following the first special session on disarmament. Due to divergent views regarding the question of possible assistance to South Africa in the nuclear field and the scope of the proposed sanctions, the Commission has been unable to agree on a text of recommendations.

B. THE BALKANS

The establishment of a nuclear-weapon-free zone in the Balkans has been the subject of several initiatives and specific proposals put forward by various States. As early as September 1957, Romania proposed the establishment of an area of peace in the Balkans free of foreign military bases. The idea was subsequently further detailed by Romania and taken up by other countries as well, including the Soviet Union. Thus, in 1959, the USSR suggested that the Balkan peninsula be made a region of peace, without any missiles or nuclear weapons. On various occasions the Balkan countries, including Albania, Bulgaria, Romania and Yugoslavia, expressed support and interest in the zone specifying at the same time some of their concerns and ideas on the modalities and scope of such a zone.

Since the beginning of the 1980s, the idea of inter-Balkan co-operation for creating a nuclear-weapon-free zone has once again become the focus of intensified public and governmental attention in most of the countries of the region. Thus, at summit meetings held in 1982, 1983 and 1984, Bulgaria, Greece, Romania and Yugoslavia supported in their joint statements and declarations the transformation of the Balkans into a nuclear-weapon-free zone, or into a zone of peace and co-operation free of nuclear weapons, and made suggestions for elaborating a nuclear-weapon-free status for the Balkans. While attaching great importance to the transformation of the Balkans into a zone of peace and co-operation free from nuclear weapons, Yugoslavia has considered that the success of such a proposal depends on the overall situation in the broader region of the Mediterranean and Europe. Turkey, for its part, in expressing its support for the concept of zones of peace and nuclear-weapon-free zones wherever possible and feasible, has noted that the security of the Balkans is directly related to that of Europe as a whole and that one cannot be separated from the other.

At the initiative of Greece, a conference of governmental experts from Bulgaria, Greece, Romania, Turkey and Yugoslavia was held in Athens in January/February 1984 with an agenda which included the question of the establishment of a nuclear-weapon-free zone in the Balkans. It was agreed by the experts that the ideas, proposals and suggestions which were registered during the Conference would be submitted for consideration of the Governments of the participating States in order to continue the dialogue started at that Conference. It was the first meeting in Europe of governmental experts representing States belonging to different military alliances or having non-aligned status that discussed proposals for the establishment of a nuclear-weapon-free zone in the Balkans.

C. Central Europe

Proposals for a nuclear-weapon-free zone in Central Europe were put forward on numerous occasions in the 1950s. In March 1956, the Soviet Union proposed in the Disarmament Commission that a zone be created in Central Europe where armaments would be subject to limitation and inspection and the stationing of any atomic or hydrogen weapons would be prohibited. Poland formally put forward in the General Assembly a proposal for a nuclear-weapon-free zone (Rapacki Plan), first in 1957 and again in 1958. The latter version provided for a nuclear-weapon-free zone covering Poland, Czechoslovakia, the Democratic Republic of Germany and the Federal Republic of Germany. According to the plan, there would be no nuclear weapons in that area; the use of such weapons against it would be forbidden and a broad system of control would be introduced.

The proposal was supported by socialist countries. Western countries, for their part, objected to it on the ground that it made no reference to limiting conventional forces and involved a variety of political and strategic problems closely related to the geographical area covered. These comments reflected differences between NATO and the parties to the Warsaw Treaty concerning major political and strategic issues such as the German problem, the military balance in Europe, the introduction of tactical and medium-range nuclear weapons and NATO's plans to create multinational nuclear forces.

In order to meet some of the Western objections, Poland submitted two more versions of the plan to the ENDC in 1962. The revisions provided, among other things, for the reduction of some conventional forces. In 1964, without withdrawing the Rapacki Plan, Poland submitted a new plan (Gomulka Plan), which did not call for an immediate reduction of the nuclear weapons already deployed within the zone, but envisaged a freeze at the existing level; in addition, an extensive system of verification was stipulated. Since then, Poland has on various occasions reaffirmed the validity of its 1957 proposal, as developed in subsequent years, as well as that of 1964.

In 1982 the Independent Commission on Disarmament and Security Issues (the Palme Commission), convinced that there must be substantial reductions in nuclear stockpiles leading to the denuclearization of Europe, recommended the establishment of a battlefield nuclear-weapon-free zone, starting with Central Europe and extending ultimately from the northern to the southern flanks of the NATO and Warsaw Treaty alliances. This scheme was to be implemented in the context of an agreement on parity and mutual force reductions in Central Europe. No nuclear munitions were to be permitted in the zone.

More recently, in 1983, the question of establishing a nuclear-weapon-free zone in Central Europe was also discussed in the Disarmament Commission. In that context, Mexico suggested that the Disarmament Commission should endorse the proposal of the Palme Commission envisaging the creation of a battlefield nuclear-weapon-free zone in Central Europe. Mexico then called on the members of the two military alliances to begin negotiations on the issue without further delay. This proposal was supported by a number of delegations, but others raised objections to it on various grounds. Due to these differences, the Disarmament Commission recommended that the proposal be duly taken into account in ongoing and future disarmament efforts.

D. Middle East

The danger of nuclear-weapon proliferation posed by the greater access of States to nuclear technology and particularly the danger of the rapid diffusion of such technology within the political setting of the Middle East led Iran, in 1974, to ask the General Assembly to consider the question of establishing a denuclearized zone in the Middle East. Egypt subsequently co-sponsored the request.

The proposal to establish such a zone was supported by most States of the region and the first resolution on the question was adopted by the Assembly on 9 December 1974. By the resolution, the Assembly commended the idea of establishing a nuclear-weapon-free zone in the Middle East and considered that it was indispensable that all concerned parties in the area "proclaim solemnly and immediately their intention to refrain, on a reciprocal basis, from producing, testing, obtaining, acquiring or in any other way possessing nuclear weapons". It also called upon the States concerned, that had not yet done so, to accede to the non-proliferation Treaty. In pursuance of that resolution, the Secretary-General invited views and ideas from those States and subsequently submitted a report containing the responses received.

Each year between 1975 and 1984, the General Assembly has adopted resolutions on this issue. Since its 1980 session, they have been adopted by consensus.

Recently there has been increasing concern about Israel's reported nuclear-weapon capability. Thus, in 1979, the General Assembly requested the Secretary-General to undertake a study on the issue. The study, *Israeli Nuclear Armament*, submitted by the Secretary-General to the General Assembly in 1981, concluded that there was widespread agreement among technical experts that, given Israel's nuclear activities and level of expertise, it was capable of manufacturing nuclear explosive devices and possessed the means of delivery of such weapons to targets in the area, but the experts were unable to conclude definitely whether or not Israel was currently in possession of nuclear weapons. The study also stated that "the possession of nuclear weapons by Israel would be a serious destabilizing factor in the already tense situation prevailing in the Middle East, in addition to being a serious danger to the cause of non-proliferation in general".

The proposal for the creation of a nuclear-weapon-free zone in the Middle East has met with wide acceptance in the General Assembly and over a period of several years it has enjoyed wide support in the region itself.

E. MEDITERRANEAN

On 27 May 1963, the USSR submitted to the ENDC a proposal suggesting that the whole Mediterranean area should be declared a zone free of nuclear weapons. Subsequently, the Soviet Union and the States parties to the Warsaw Treaty have made proposals aimed at eliminating nuclear weapons from the Mediterranean. Some States bordering the Mediterranean seem to have given high priority to proposals for the establishment of nuclear-weapon-free zones in that area. Other States concerned have adopted a more general approach directed towards the transformation of the Mediterranean into a region of peace, security and co-operation, free from confrontation and conflict. Still others, such as Italy and France, have stated that security in the Mediterranean is inseparable from European security as a whole. Thus, in the view of these States, any disarmament measure envisaged for the Mediterranean should be precisely defined and cannot be undertaken in isolation from disarmament measures for all of Europe.

The various approaches are summarized in the analytical report of the Secretary-General on the strengthening of security and co-operation in the Mediterranean region, based on replies from 27 Governments, which he submitted to the General Assembly in 1983.

They are also reflected in the resolutions entitled "Strengthening of security and co-operation in the Mediterranean region", adopted without a vote by the General Assembly in 1983 and in 1984.

F. NORTHERN EUROPE

The idea of establishing a nuclear-weapon-free zone in Northern Europe was first suggested by the Soviet Union in 1958. That idea was followed up in several subsequent statements by Soviet officials indicating support for a nuclear-weapon-free zone in the Scandinavian peninsula and the Baltic area, as well as for the combining of three proposed zones — Scandinavian–Baltic, Central Europe and Balkan–Adriatic — into a single nuclear-weapon-free zone.

In the early 1960s, several suggestions were made regarding the establishment of a nuclear-weapon-free zone in the Nordic and Baltic areas. They were related in part to proposals put forward at that time for other nuclear-weapon-free zones in Europe, and in part to the consideration, in the United Nations, of the proposal submitted by Sweden (Undén Plan) for a non-nuclear club. Since 1963 the idea of establishing a nuclear-weapon-free zone in Northern Europe has been advocated most notably by Finland. It has pointed out that despite the differences in their security policies, none of the Nordic countries has acquired nuclear weapons or accepted those belonging to other States on its territory. Accordingly, a Nordic nuclear-weapon-free zone would only confirm, through mutual undertakings, the existing *de facto* situation of the absence of nuclear weapons without impairing the security of the Nordic countries or affecting the balance of power in the world (Kekkonen Plan).

The idea gained new momentum when, in 1978, Finland returned to its 1963 proposal, urging negotiations on arms regulation by the Nordic countries among themselves and together with the great Powers concerned. The objective would be a separate treaty arrangement covering the Nordic countries, which would isolate them as completely as possible from the effects of nuclear strategy in general and from nuclear weapons technology in particular. The Finnish Government has several times reiterated its position on this issue, notably in May 1983, when it stated that the idea had lost none of its validity and that Finland would continue to work for its realization. The different attitudes of the Nordic Governments have prevented the achievement of concrete results thus far. However, their foreign ministers have since 1981 discussed the question in their regular meetings.

The Soviet Union has on various occasions expressed an active interest in the establishment of the nuclear-weapon-free zone in Northern Europe. In a statement of 6 June 1983, the Soviet Union expressed its readiness to respect the status of such a zone, and also to consider the question of certain measures relating to its own territory adjacent to the zone, which would promote the strengthening of its nuclear-weapon-free status. While France has expressed a cautious attitude with regard to the proposal, due to the geo-strategic importance of the Baltic region, the other nuclear-weapon States have not specifically addressed the subject, but their generally held views on nuclear-weapon-free zones would apply equally to this region.

G. SOUTH ASIA

The Assembly first considered the question of a denuclearized zone in South Asia in 1974, at the request of Pakistan, which saw an urgent need for such a zone.

In the debate, Pakistan noted that all the States of the region had already expressed opposition to the acquisition or introduction of nuclear weapons. In particular, it pointed out that India, both before and after the 1974 explosion of its nuclear device, had indicated that it would not develop or acquire nuclear weapons.

India made clear its support for the principle of establishing nuclear-weapon-free zones, provided that suitable conditions existed in a particular region and that the proposal was initiated and agreed to by the countries of the region. India believed, however, that South Asia could not be treated in isolation, as it was only a subregion, an integral part of the region of Asia and the Pacific. The existence of nuclear weapons in the region and the presence of foreign military bases in the Indian Ocean complicated the whole security environment and made the situation inappropriate for the establishment of a nuclear-weapon-free zone there, according to India.

Two separate resolutions submitted by India and Pakistan, closely reflecting their different positions, were both approved by the General Assembly on 9 December 1974. By the resolution initiated by India, the Assembly decided to give due consideration to any proposal for the creation of a nuclear-weapon-free zone in an appropriate region of Asia, after it had been developed and matured by the countries of the region. By the resolution initiated by Pakistan, the General Assembly urged the States of South Asia to begin consultations for the purpose of establishing such a zone and, in the interim, to refrain from any actions contrary to the achievement of that objective.

Between 1975 and 1984, 11 resolutions have been adopted by large majorities on the question, two in 1975 and one each year since 1976, initiated by Pakistan alone.

During the debates in the General Assembly, since 1974, Pakistan has consistently maintained that the generally recognized conditions for the establishment of a nuclear-weapon-free zone exist in South Asia. All the States of the region have already declared their opposition to the acquisition of nuclear weapons or to their introduction into the region. The five States possessing nuclear weapons have, in principle, indicated their support for or acceptance of the concept of establishing nuclear-weapon-free zones.

India's viewpoint is that the nuclear-weapon-free zone idea has become unrealistic and that the movement and deployment of nuclear weapons in various regions of the world by the nuclear-weapon States are

102

fundamentally irreconcilable with the very idea of nuclear-weapon-free zones. At the second special session of the General Assembly on disarmament, in 1982, India's Foreign Minister stated that his country could not subscribe to the legitimization of the possession of nuclear weapons by a few Powers by agreeing to live under their professedly benign protection in the guise of a nuclear-weapon-free zone.

H. SOUTH PACIFIC

Nuclear testing in the South Pacific by some nuclear-weapon States, proposals for the storage or dumping of nuclear waste material in the Pacific Ocean, and the presence of nuclear-weapon Powers in the region have led the States of that area to seek a solution to these problems at the regional level. Thus, on the basis of an initiative of Fiji and New Zealand, the General Assembly adopted, in 1975, a resolution by which it noted that the heads of Government of the independent or self-governing States members of the South Pacific Forum had emphasized in their communiqué of 3 July 1975 the importance of keeping the South Pacific region free from the risk of nuclear contamination and of involvement in a nuclear conflict, and had commended the idea of a nuclear-weapon-free zone in the South Pacific as a means of achieving that aim. The Assembly invited the countries concerned to carry forward consultations about ways and means of realizing their objective and endorsed the idea of establishing a nuclear-weapon-free zone in the South Pacific.

Among the nuclear Powers, only China voted for the resolution. The others abstained, expressing reservations concerning the fact that such a zone would appear, necessarily, to include areas of the high seas or international straits, which could interfere with the rights of navigation.

Following the adoption of that resolution, no further action was taken regarding the initiative for a number of years, although it was occasionally recalled in the First Committee of the General Assembly.

The idea of a nuclear-weapon-free zone in the South Pacific was again high on the agenda at meetings of the South Pacific Forum in 1983 and 1984, along with the questions of the testing of nuclear weapons and the dumping of radioactive waste in that region. At the 1984 Forum, heads of Government "agreed on the desirability of establishing a nuclear-weapon-free zone in the region at the earliest possible opportunity" in accordance with a set of principles endorsed by the meeting. These principles, among others, were that the South Pacific countries should be free to live in peace and independence and to run their own affairs in accordance with the wishes and traditions of their people; South Pacific countries should enjoy peaceful social and economic development free from the threat of environmental pollution; there should be no use, testing or stationing of nuclear explosive devices in the South Pacific; and no South Pacific country would develop or manufacture, or receive from others, or acquire or test any nuclear explosive device.

The Forum appointed a working group of officials to undertake an examination of the substantive legal and other issues involved in establishing a nuclear-free zone in the region.

Zones of peace

The establishment of zones of peace is a relatively new concept, developed in response to growing regional tensions and conflicts and increasing military presence of major Powers in various seas and oceans in the world. The 1978 Final Document of the special session on disarmament stated that the establishment of zones of peace in various regions of the world under appropriate conditions, to be clearly defined and determined freely by the States concerned in the zone, taking into account the characteristics of the zone and the principles of the Charter of the United Nations, and in conformity with international law, could contribute to strengthening the security of States within such zones and to international peace and security as a whole (paragraph 64).

INDIAN OCEAN

One such proposal on the agenda of the United Nations deals with the establishment of a zone of peace in the Indian Ocean. It first gained prominence when a conference of heads of State or Government of non-aligned countries meeting in Lusaka in September 1970 endorsed the idea and called upon the United Nations to declare the Indian Ocean a zone of peace, from which great-Power rivalries, military bases and nuclear weapons would be excluded.

As a direct result of that action, the General Assembly, at the initiative of Sri Lanka, later joined by the United Republic of Tanzania, adopted a resolution in 1971 by which it solemnly declared that the Indian Ocean, within limits to be determined, was designated for all time as a zone of peace. In conformity with the Declaration it called on the great Powers to enter into consultations with the littoral States with a view to halting the further expansion of their military presence in the Indian Ocean and eliminating from the area all their bases, military installations, nuclear weapons, and weapons of mass destruction and any manifestation of great-Power rivalry. It also called upon the littoral and hinterland States, the permanent members of the Security Council and other major maritime users of the Indian Ocean to enter into consultations, with a view to implementing the Declaration of the Indian Ocean as a Zone of Peace and ensuring that:

(a) Warships and military aircraft would not use the Indian Ocean for any threat or use of force against any of its littoral and hinterland States;

(*b*) Subject to the foregoing and to the norms and principles of international law, the right to free and unimpeded use of the zone by all nations would be unaffected;

(*c*) Arrangements would be made to give effect to any international agreement ultimately reached on the question.

The resolution was adopted by a vote of 60 to none, with 55 abstentions, thus reflecting widely divergent views between non-aligned States and major military Powers regarding practical aspects and implications of the Declaration.

In 1972, the General Assembly established a 15-member *Ad Hoc* Committee on the Indian Ocean (increased to 18 members in 1974, 23 in 1977, 45 in 1980 and 48 in 1984) to study the implications of the proposal with specific reference to the practical measures that might be taken in furtherance of the objective of the Declaration. Since 1973, consideration in the General Assembly has generally centered on the report of the *Ad Hoc* Committee.

Concurrently, the Conference of Heads of State or Government of Non-Aligned Countries, meeting in Algiers in 1973, in Colombo in 1976, in Havana in 1979 and in New Delhi in 1983, have consistently reaffirmed support for the concept of the Indian Ocean as a zone of peace and have actively searched for ways to promote its effective implementation.

In addition, bilateral Soviet-American talks were initiated in 1977 to pursue possible limitations on military activities in the Indian Ocean. Three rounds of talks were held in 1977 and 1978, but the talks were suspended in February of that year. In an agreed statement submitted to the Chairman of the *Ad Hoc* Committee on 1 March 1978, the United States and the Soviet Union stated that there had been to date a certain measure of agreement on a number of questions, including the desirability of a staged approach, beginning with an agreement not to increase the current military presence, then moving on promptly to negotiations on reductions. The bilateral talks had not resumed by March 1985.

The question of the Indian Ocean as a zone of peace was given considerable attention in the course of the preparation for the 1978 first special session of the General Assembly devoted to disarmament, as well as at the special session itself. Various proposals on the subject were submitted, raising such issues as the need for prompt measures to implement the Declaration of the Indian Ocean as a Zone of Peace; the necessity for mutual restraint on the part of the littoral and hinterland States, as well as the maintenance of a reasonable military balance among themselves; and the need for the convening of a Conference on the Indian Ocean. At the special session considerable time and effort were devoted to the question, but there was no progress on the outstanding issues concerning the implementation of the Declaration.

In 1979, a Meeting of the Littoral and Hinterland States, which the members of the *Ad Hoc* Committee, the great Powers and the major maritime users of the Indian Ocean attended, was held in New York. In its Final Document, that Meeting recommended the holding of the Conference on the Indian Ocean, and proposed that the *Ad Hoc* Committee on the Indian Ocean undertake the preparatory work for it, including consideration of appropriate arrangements for any international agreement that might ultimately be reached.

The same year, the General Assembly decided to convene the Conference on the Indian Ocean in 1981 at Colombo, Sri Lanka, and to enlarge the *Ad Hoc* Committee further, inviting the permanent members of the Security Council and major maritime users of the Indian Ocean to participate in it. However, during 1980 and 1981, the *Ad Hoc* Committee was unable to make definitive progress in the preparations for the Conference or to finalize dates for its convening. Each year since then, the Committee has been requested to make every effort to accomplish the necessary preparatory work for the Conference, including, specifically, the finalization of dates.

During its first session in 1984, the work of the Committee was devoted to the framework of the provisional agenda for the Conference, the provisional rules of procedure and substantive issues related to a zone of peace in the Indian Ocean area. Most of the non-aligned States and the Eastern European States maintained that, notwithstanding the necessity of continuing the harmonization of views on the substantive issues related to a zone of peace in the Indian Ocean, those issues should be solved at the Conference itself and should not be a pre-condition for convening the Conference. The Western States emphasized that until the necessary harmonization of views on the substantive issues related to a zone of peace had been achieved, particularly the fundamental characteristics of such a zone, it would be premature to convene the Conference. Since in 1984 the Committee was unable to complete the preparatory work for the Conference, the General Assembly, by consensus, requested the *Ad Hoc* Committee to complete the preparatory work in 1985 in order to enable the opening of the Conference in the first half of 1986, taking into account the political and security climate in the region and in consultation with the host country.

Chapter VIII

Other weapons of mass destruction

The efforts of the United Nations in the field of disarmament have not been limited to nuclear weapons. Indeed, the General Assembly, in its often cited first resolution, of 24 January 1946, envisaged not only the elimination from national armaments of atomic weapons, but also "of all other major weapons adaptable to mass destruction".

A general definition of weapons of mass destruction was given as early as 1948 by the Commission for Conventional Armaments, a subsidiary body of the Security Council which functioned from 1947 to 1950. In August of that year, the Commission adopted a resolution which stated that "weapons of mass destruction should be defined to include atomic explosive weapons, radioactive material weapons, lethal chemical and biological weapons, and any weapons developed in the future which have characteristics comparable in destructive effect to those of the atomic bomb or other weapons mentioned above". Thus, over the years, efforts were made to ban chemical and biological weapons through an international convention.

Chemical weapons were widely used in the First World War. According to official reports, gas casualties numbered about 1,300,000, of which about 100,000 were fatal. A powerful sense of outrage generated by the use of such weapons resulted in the adoption, at Geneva in 1925, of the Protocol for the Prohibition of the Use in War of Asphyxiating, Poisonous or Other Gases, and of Bacteriological Methods of Warfare. This pioneer arms limitation agreement has been in existence for more than half a century, and at the end of 1984, 105 States were parties to it. The Protocol prohibits "the use in war of asphyxiating, poisonous or other gases, and of all analogous liquids, materials or devices" as well as "bacteriological methods of warfare". It does not prohibit the development, production or stockpiling of such weapons, however. Consequently, many of its adherents attached statements to the effect that they might use such weapons if they were first used against them, and the Protocol does not provide an overall solution to the question.

The agents concerned are usually described in terms of their physiological effects and are characterized as follows:

(a) Nerve agents are colourless, odourless, tasteless chemicals of the same family as organophosphorus insecticides. They poison the nervous system and disrupt vital body functions. They constitute the most modern war chemicals known; they kill quickly and are more potent than are any other chemical agents (except toxins);

(b) Blister agents (vesicants) are oily liquids which, in the main, burn and blister the skin within hours after exposure. They also have general toxic effects. Blister agents caused more casualties than any other chemical agent used in the First World War;

(c) Choking agents are highly volatile liquids which, when breathed as gases, irritate and severely injure the lungs, causing death from choking. They were introduced in the First World War and are of much lower potency than the nerve agents;

(d) Blood agents are also intended to enter the body through the respiratory tract. They produce death by interfering with the utilization of oxygen by the tissues. They, too, are much less toxic than nerve agents;

(e) Tear and harassing gases are sensory irritants which cause a temporary flow of tears, irritation of the skin and respiratory tract and, occasionally, nausea and vomiting. They have been widely used as riot-control agents and also in war;

(f) Psycho-chemicals are drug-like chemicals intended to cause temporary mental disturbances;

(g) Herbicides (defoliants) are agricultural chemicals which poison or desiccate the leaves of plants, causing them to lose their leaves or die. Some herbicides, particularly those containing organic arsenic, are also toxic for man and animals.

The question of chemical weapons and chemical warfare was considered intermittently in the 1950s and 1960s, usually in conjunction with biological weapons and also as one aspect of various comprehensive disarmament proposals. One issue that has for some time impeded progress on the question was whether chemical and bacteriological (biological) weapons should be considered jointly.

In 1968, the General Assembly requested the Secretary-General to prepare, with the assistance of qualified experts, a report on chemical and bacteriological weapons. According to the report, entitled *Chemical and Bacteriological (Biological) Weapons and the Effects of Their Possible Use*, while all weapons of war are destructive of human life, "chemical and bacteriological (biological) weapons stand in a class of their own as armaments which exercise their effects solely on living matter". In addition, the experts observed "that certain chemical and bacteriological (biological) agents are potentially unconfined in their effects, both in space and time" and that "their large-scale use could conceivably have deleterious and irreversible effects on the balance of nature".

The following year, in 1969, the matter was discussed in the General Assembly for the first time under a separate agenda item. A draft convention on chemical and bacteriological (biological) weapons was submitted by the socialist countries at that session and then, the following year, presented to the ENDC. Also in 1969, the United Kingdom submitted to the ENDC a draft convention which dealt with the elimination of bacteriological (biological) weapons as distinct from chemical weapons. The supporters of that approach maintained that immediate agreement could be possible on a ban on that aspect of the question, while negotiations concerning the remaining problems in connection with chemical weapons could be pursued separately.

The Soviet Union and several other ENDC members, including socialist and non-aligned countries, opposed the partial approach mostly because they felt that a separate consideration of two related types of weapons was both undesirable and unwarranted. In their opinion, a separate approach to biological weapons would delay the solution of the question of chemical weapons.

These two approaches were reflected in the debates on the matter until 1971, when agreement on separating the two issues was reached. In agreeing to this separation, the Soviet Union and other socialist countries in the CCD stated that they considered the conclusion of a convention on the prohibition of the development, production and stockpiling of bacteriological (biological) and toxin weapons and on their destruction only as a first step in the search for a comprehensive solution of the problem.

Biological weapons

Following the 1971 agreement, the group of socialist States in the CCD submitted a draft convention on the prohibition of the development, production and stockpiling of bacteriological (biological) and toxin weapons and on their destruction. Later the same year, both the United States and the Soviet Union submitted to the CCD identical revised drafts of the text of such a convention. After further discussion, a single draft was submitted by socialist and Western States to the General Assembly, which subsequently commended the Convention and requested the depositary Governments, the Soviet Union, the United Kingdom and the United States, to open it for signature and ratification at the earliest possible date.

The Convention on the Prohibition of the Development, Production and Stockpiling of Bacteriological (Biological) and Toxin Weapons and on Their Destruction was opened for signature on 10 April 1972 and entered into force on 26 March 1975. By the end of 1984, the Convention had been ratified by 100 countries.

The parties to the Convention undertake never in any circumstances to develop, produce, stockpile or otherwise acquire or retain: (*a*) microbial or other biological agents, or toxins whatever their origin or method of production, of types and in quantities that have no justification for prophylactic, protective or other peaceful purposes; or (b) weapons, equipment or means of delivery designed to use such agents or toxins for hostile purposes or in armed conflict (article I).

Each State party to the Convention undertakes to destroy or to divert to peaceful purposes all agents, toxins, weapons, equipment and means of delivery specified, which are in its possession or under its jurisdiction or control (article II).

Any State party which finds that any other State party is not complying with the provisions of the Convention may lodge a complaint with the Security Council of the United Nations. Each State party also undertakes to co-operate in carrying out any investigation which the Security Council may initiate, in accordance with the provisions of the Charter of the United Nations, on the basis of the complaint received by the Council (article VI).

The Convention, furthermore, contains a provision stating that each party undertakes to continue negotiations in good faith with a view to reaching an early agreement on effective measures for the prohibition of the development, production and stockpiling of chemical weapons and for their destruction, and on appropriate measures concerning their equipment and means of delivery (article IX).

The First Review Conference of the parties to the biological weapons Convention was held in 1980, five years after its entry into force. The Conference was convened pursuant to article XII, which provides for such a review in order to ensure that the purposes of the preamble and provisions of the Convention are being realized. In the Final Declaration, the participating States reaffirmed the strong support of the parties for the Convention and for the effective implementation of all its provisions. They regretted, however, that no agreement had yet been achieved for the prohibition of the development, production and stockpiling of chemical weapons, as foreseen by the Convention itself. They were on the whole satisfied with the implementation of the Convention at that time and called for greater efforts to increase scientific and technical co-operation, particularly with developing countries, in the peaceful uses of biological agents and toxins.

Chemical weapons

Since 1971, the question of chemical weapons has been independently considered in the multilateral negotiating body in Geneva. The discussions have involved a number of highly complicated issues. Of primary importance among them has been the question of the scope of the prohibition, whether or not its full implementation should be immediate or spread over a period of time, and to what activities and agents it would apply. Another question, that of verification methods, has focused particularly on the issue of on-site verification procedures, whether they should be systematic, by challenge, or a combination of the two, to whatever extent necessary to supplement national technical means.

In 1974, the Soviet Union and the United States announced to the CCD that they had agreed in principle to consider a joint initiative with respect to the conclusion of an international convention dealing with the most dangerous lethal means of chemical warfare. Following that, and through 1980 (but not since then), bilateral negotiations on the question were held between the two Powers in an effort to reach agreement on a text. Joint reports to the Committee on Disarmament on the progress achieved in the negotiations were submitted in 1979 and in 1980. Although the 1980 report was quite extensive and showed considerable progress, various members of the Committee still felt the pace of negotiations was inadequate.

At the first special session of the General Assembly devoted to disarmament, in 1978, the Assembly emphasized that the conclusion of an agreement banning chemical weapons was one of the most urgent tasks of multilateral negotiations and that, after its conclusion, all States should contribute to ensuring its broadest possible application through early signature and ratification.

In 1980, in an effort to make greater progress, the Committee on Disarmament decided to establish an *ad hoc* working group on chemical weapons with a mandate to define issues to be dealt with in the negotiations on a convention banning chemical weapons, and negotiations have been undertaken in that body ever since. For this purpose it has been re-established every year. While there is general agreement that a convention should be comprehensive in scope and should, therefore, provide for the destruction of current stockpiles and the dismantling of production and storage facilities, differences of approach have persisted. Such differences centre on the assurance of the non-production of chemical weapons in the chemical industry and appropriate verification measures to guarantee compliance.

The General Assembly has repeatedly called for a resumption of the bilateral negotiations between the USSR and the United States. It has also called upon all States, although these resolutions have not been adopted by consensus, to refrain from the production and development of binary and other more modern types of chemical weapons, as well as from stationing chemical weapons in States where such weapons have not yet been introduced. The United States, among others, has regarded the last-mentioned approach as one-sided, in that it singles out one type of chemical weapon and speaks of chemical-weapon-free zones even though such weapons could be easily reintroduced into such zones.

At the second special session of the General Assembly devoted to disarmament, in 1982, the Soviet Union for the first time submitted the basic provisions of a convention which provided for the possibility of systematic on-site inspection of the destruction of stocks of chemical weapons and of the production, for permitted purposes, of supertoxic lethal chemicals at specified facilities. The United States, however, still regarded the position of the USSR on verification issues as unclear, and put forward, as minimum requirements, systematic on-site verification of: (a) destruction of stockpiles on a continuous basis, (b) disposition of production facilities, and (c) permitted small-scale production of lethal chemicals. The Soviet proposal was later submitted to the Committee on Disarmament.

Early in 1984, the United States presented to the Conference on Disarmament a draft treaty which entailed a complete world-wide ban on chemical weapons with a verification system based on the concept of "open invitation". Parties would also be obliged to declare within 30 days all chemical-weapon stocks, production facilities and past transfers, with destruction of stocks and of production facilities to begin within 1 year and to be completed within 10 years of the entry into force of the treaty. In keeping with the draft's concept of verification, a consultative committee would be established to oversee the implementation of the convention and would conduct mandatory on-site verification. Special on-site inspections with only 24-hour notice are also envisaged in the United States draft.

The USSR and other socialist countries rejected the United States approach to verification and stressed that the United States draft could only serve to hamper progress in the elaboration of a convention. In August 1984, the Soviet Union and other socialist States submitted a working paper to the Conference entitled "The organization and functioning of the Consultative Committee", which envisaged that this body, *inter alia*, would regulate both international systematic on-site inspections and on-site inspections by challenge.

Another element was added to the discussions in 1980, when the General Assembly, by its resolution 35/144 C, adopted by a vote of 78 to 17, with 36 abstentions, decided to carry out an impartial investigation to ascertain the facts pertaining to reports alleging that chemical weapons had been used in recent wars and certain military operations in various regions of the world. The Secretary-General was then requested to carry out such an investigation with the assistance of qualified medical and technical experts and to report to the Assembly. The Group of Experts established in 1981 submitted a final report to the General Assembly in 1982. As reflected in it, due to circumstances beyond its control, the Group was not in a position to proceed to the territories where chemical attacks had allegedly occurred and it was, therefore, unable to conduct any on-site investigations. In the end, "while the Group could not state that those allegations had been proven, nevertheless, it could not disregard the circumstantial evidence suggestive of the possible use of some sort of toxic chemical substance in some instances".

'A draft resolution taking note of that report was introduced by New Zealand on behalf of other Western countries at the regular session of the General Assembly, in 1982. During the debate, the United States said that the qualified language of the experts was not surprising because they had been denied access to the territories concerned. The United States held, however, that the material compiled by the Group supported its own finding of the identification of toxic agents in samples. The Soviet Union, noting that from the beginning it had been against the establishment of the Group of Experts, which it regarded as designed to poison the international political atmosphere, stated that the report of the experts had not confirmed the allegations relating to cases of the use of chemical weapons. The General Assembly adopted the draft resolution by a recorded vote of 83 to 22, with 33 abstentions, as resolution 37/98 E.

Furthermore, in 1982, the General Assembly adopted resolution 37/98 D by a vote of 86 to 19, with 33 abstentions, by which the Secretary-General was requested to investigate, with the assistance of qualified experts, information that might be brought to his attention by any Member State concerning activities that might constitute a violation of the Protocol or of the relevant rules of customary international law in order to ascertain the facts of the matter, and promptly report the results of any such investigation to all Member States and to the General Assembly. In addition, the Secretary-General was requested to compile and maintain lists of qualified experts and of laboratories and to devise, with the assistance of qualified consultant experts, procedures for the timely and effective investigation of information concerning the above-mentioned activities.

The report of the Group of Consultant Experts on Provisional Procedures to Uphold the Authority of the 1925 Geneva Protocol, established in 1982 by the Assembly in accordance with resolution 37/98 D, mentioned above, was completed in 1984. The body of the report consists of three main parts: (a) procedures devised by the Group of Experts (criteria to guide the Secretary-General in deciding whether or not to initiate an investigation; follow-up actions related to the initiation of an investigation; specific guidance for the conduct of an investigation; and specific tasks relating to the organization and conduct of an investigation); (b) assembling and systematic organization of documentation; and (c) administrative support for implementing and updating the procedures. The report included ten appendices.

In 1984, in response to a request by the Islamic Republic of Iran, which in a number of communications to the United Nations in 1983 and early 1984 had alleged that chemical weapons were being used by Iraq, the Secretary-General requested four eminent specialists to undertake a fact-finding visit to Iran to determine, as far as possible, whether chemical weapons had been used and, if so, their type and the extent of their use. The specialists spent six days in Iran, from 13 to 19 March, and reached the following unanimous conclusions in their report:

"Chemical weapons in the form of aerial bombs have been used in the areas inspected in Iran by the specialists."

In March 1984, the Security Council took note of the report of the specialists and declared, among other things, that it strongly condemned the use of chemical weapons and that it reaffirmed the need to abide strictly by the provisions of the Geneva Protocol of 1925.

The General Assembly, for its part, in all recent years, including its 1984 regular session, has urged the Conference on Disarmament to intensify negotiations on a convention banning chemical weapons and has several times requested that its subsidiary body proceed immediately to the drafting of such a convention.

New types of weapons of mass destruction and new systems of such weapons; radiological weapons

The question of new weapons of mass destruction has been under continuous consideration in the General Assembly and in the Conference on Disarmament for a number of years. The item "Prohibition of the development and manufacture of new types of weapons of mass destruction and new systems of such weapons" was first included in the agenda of the General Assembly in 1975 at the initiative of the Soviet Union, which submitted a draft international agreement. The topic is at present on the agenda of the Conference on Disarmament.

The Soviet Union and other socialist States in the Conference advocate a general prohibition of the development of new types and systems of weapons of mass destruction, on the ground that it is always more difficult to eliminate weapons after they are deployed than to ban their development and manufacture. With respect to the scope of the prohibition, those States have suggested that new types of weapons of mass destruction should include any type of weapon based on qualitatively new principles of action with regard to method of use, the target to be attacked or the nature of impact. Most Western countries, while agreeing that the subject should be kept under review, have taken a different approach, namely, that new scientific developments should be dealt with individually as they arise and appear to have a weapons potential. They have also held that the various developments pointed out by the Eastern European States as potential new weapons of mass destruction fall within categories that have already been identified and should be covered in that context, rather than as new weapons of mass destruction.

The Final Document of the 1978 special session of the General Assembly stated in paragraph 77 that in order to help prevent a qualitative arms race and so that scientific and technological achievements might ultimately be used solely for peaceful purposes, effective measures should be taken to avoid the danger and prevent the emergence of new types of weapons of mass destruction based on new scientific principles and achievements. The same year, the General Assembly, at its regular session, adopted two separate resolutions on the issue, one sponsored by the Western States and the other by the Eastern European States, reflecting the respective approaches.

Subsequently, the Soviet Union clarified its position by calling for a comprehensive agreement on the prohibition of new weapons of mass destruction that would be accompanied by a list of specific types to be banned, with the possibility of adding to the list in the future and the possibility of concluding separate agreements on specific new types of weapons as they emerged. To that end, in 1979, the Soviet Union submitted a document to the Committee on Disarmament in which it listed some types of potential weapons of mass destruction, such as:

(*a*) Radiological weapons (using radioactive materials) which could produce harmful radiation effects similar to effects of a nuclear explosion;

(*b*) Particle-beam weapons based on the use of charged or neutral particles to affect biological targets. Sufficiently powerful bundles of particles could be produced in accelerators used for research; in some operating accelerators, the energy of accelerated particles attained hundreds of millions of electron volts. Reduction of the size and weight of accelerator systems and power sources could permit their use as weapons;

(*c*) Infrasonic "acoustic radiation" weapons. They would utilize harmful effects of infrasonic oscillations on biocurrents of the brain and nervous system;

(*d*) Electromagnetic weapons operating at certain radio-frequency radiations, which could have injurious effects on human organs. Within a few years, devices capable of directional transmission of electromagnetic radiation of enormous power over distances of several hundred kilometres might be developed, and radiation density in excess of safety standards could be produced over areas measuring dozens of square kilometres.

In response, the United States and other Western countries, while expressing readiness to work out agreements on specific types of weapons which might be identified, took the position that a single treaty on the subject of all potential new weapons of mass destruction would have to be so general in its scope and so vague in its definitions that it would not be effective.

Every year since 1979, the General Assembly, on the initiative of Eastern European and non-aligned States, has adopted resolutions on the issue which, in the light of the different positions held, have not received the support of Western States in the voting. In its resolutions, the

Assembly, among other things, has requested the negotiating body in Geneva to conduct negotiations, with the assistance of qualified governmental experts, with a view to preparing a draft comprehensive agreement on the prohibition of the development and manufacture of new types of weapons of mass destruction and new systems of such weapons and, where necessary, specific agreements on particular types of such weapons. Since 1981, the General Assembly has further called upon the permanent members of the Security Council and other militarily important States to make declarations renouncing the creation of new types and systems of weapons of mass destruction, to be subsequently approved by the Security Council.

In the Committee on Disarmament, the issue was discussed mainly during plenary meetings. In 1981 and 1982, periodic informal meetings were held with the participation of experts in order to identify cases which might require particular consideration and which would justify the opening of specific negotiations.

At its 1983 and 1984 sessions, that negotiating body discussed the question at plenary meetings and intends to do so in 1985. The item under which the matter is considered is entitled: "New types of weapons of mass destruction and new systems of such weapons; radiological weapons". The Soviet Union and other socialist States have stressed the need for an *ad hoc* group of qualified governmental experts to elaborate both a general agreement and separate agreements on specific new weapons of mass destruction. Western States, while restating their views on the matter, have pointed out anew that no such weapon has been identified so far and that the so-called nuclear neutron bomb, for example, about which concern has been expressed, could not be considered as a new weapon as it is clearly a nuclear weapon and not based on new scientific principles. During the debate it has also been suggested that the more powerfully armed States should adopt unilateral measures to prevent the use of scientific and technical discoveries for military purposes. Because of these differences of approach, it has not been possible to establish an *ad hoc* group or other subsidiary body of governmental experts.

As regards radiological weapons, already in 1948 radioactive material weapons were considered to be among the potential "weapons of mass destruction", and were included in the definition of such weapons given at the time by the Commission for Conventional Armaments.

Radiological weapons, as they are usually referred to, have been described by some as weapons which could make use of the dispersal of radioactive substances in the target area to cause injury to persons independently of nuclear explosions. Although such weapons are not known to have been developed, the international community is endeavouring to ban them as potential weapons of mass destruction before they are manufactured.

The question of banning such weapons has been considered by the General Assembly at various times since 1969. That year, on the initiative of Malta, the Assembly adopted a resolution in which it recommended that the CCD consider the need for effective methods of control of nuclear weapons that maximized radioactive effects and also effective methods of control against the use of radiological methods of warfare conducted independently of nuclear explosions. The Conference reported in 1970 that it did not regard the possibility of radiological warfare as of much practical significance and did not recommend further consideration of the issue at that time.

The subject was raised again in the General Assembly by the United States in 1976. As a result of that initiative, in 1977 the United States and the USSR began bilateral negotiations on the issue of radiological weapons and the question was also considered in the CCD. The following year, the Final Document of the first special session on disarmament (paragraph 76) stated that a convention should be concluded prohibiting the development, production, stockpiling and use of radiological weapons.

A substantive development took place in 1979, when the Soviet Union and the United States submitted an agreed joint proposal to the Committee on Disarmament. As a result, in 1980, the Committee decided to establish an *ad hoc* working group on radiological weapons with a view to reaching agreement on a convention prohibiting their development, production, stockpiling and use.

During the course of deliberations in the Working Group, differences arose, however, regarding approach, priority, definitions and verification, among others. Furthermore, in 1981, Sweden called attention to the risk of mass destruction from the dissemination of radioactive substances through military attacks on civilian nuclear power installations. A number of both socialist and Western States had doubts about the feasibility of incorporating such a consideration into a radiological weapons convention, while support for the Swedish position came mostly from the group of 21 in the Committee. In order to try to resolve the new consideration generated by the Swedish proposal, the *Ad Hoc* Working Group in 1982 undertook separate consideration of the two aspects of the question, namely, the radiological weapons and the issue of military attacks on nuclear power installations. In both 1982 and 1983, progress was limited, although the Committee has continued to examine both aspects.

In 1984, the *Ad Hoc* Committee on Radiological Weapons established by the Conference on Disarmament agreed that it would consider the question of radiological weapons and the issue of attacks against nuclear facilities without setting up two separate sub-bodies to deal with them, and decided to devote two meetings to the question of linkage between the two aspects of the question. The *Ad Hoc* Committee substantively discussed and examined various documents but was not able to conclude its work and recommended that it be re-established at the beginning of 1985.

Chapter IX

Outer space

The United Nations has considered the question of outer space since the very beginning of the space age, in the late 1950s. As early as 1957, proposals were made in the Disarmament Commission to establish an inspection system that would ensure that the launching of objects through outer space would be exclusively for peaceful and scientific purposes. Growing interest in the matter led to the establishment the following year of the *Ad Hoc* Committee on the Peaceful Uses of Outer Space and to thorough discussions on the issue in the General Assembly. In 1959, as a result of the report of the *Ad Hoc* Committee, the Assembly decided to set up a permanent committee on outer space.

In the next few years, the matter continued to be the subject of debate and in 1961 the General Assembly formulated principles for the guidance of States in the exploration and use of outer space. Those principles were embodied in a resolution adopted by consensus, stating that: (*a*) international law, including the Charter of the United Nations, applied to outer space and celestial bodies and (*b*) outer space and celestial bodies were free for exploration and use by all States in conformity with international law and not subject to national appropriation. Those principles were subsequently expanded in a resolution adopted by the Assembly in 1963 also by consensus.

Discussions in 1964 focused on the legal problems involved in the exploration and use of outer space, particularly those concerning: (*a*) legal principles governing the activities of States in outer space; (*b*) assistance to and return of astronauts and space vehicles; and (*c*) liability for space vehicle accidents. The General Assembly also requested that the *Ad Hoc* Committee on the Peaceful Uses of Outer Space continue its efforts to prepare draft international agreements on those issues. On 9 May 1966, the United States requested the Chairman of the Committee to convene its legal Sub-Committee at an early date for discussion of a treaty governing the exploration of the Moon and other celestial bodies. The Soviet Union thereafter requested that an item entitled "Conclusion of an international treaty on principles governing the activities of States in the exploration and use of outer space, the Moon and other celestial bodies" be included in the agenda of the 1966 session of the General Assembly. Both the Soviet Union and the United States submitted draft treaties to

119

the Sub-Committee on 16 June. Discussions in that body led to the presentation in the First Committee of the text of a draft treaty mutually agreed upon by the two major Powers. The resolution commending the Treaty on Principles Governing the Activities of States in the Exploration and Use of Outer Space, including the Moon and Other Celestial Bodies, was sponsored by 43 Member States and unanimously adopted by the General Assembly on 19 December 1966.

According to article I of the Treaty, the exploration and use of outer space, including the Moon and other celestial bodies, is to be carried out for the benefit and in the interests of all countries, irrespective of their degree of economic or scientific development, and is to be the province of all mankind. The basic disarmament provisions of the Treaty are contained in article IV, which declares that States parties undertake not to place in orbit around the Earth any objects carrying nuclear weapons or any other kinds of weapons of mass destruction, install such weapons on celestial bodies or station them in outer space in any other manner. Article IV also affirms that the Moon and other celestial bodies are to be used exclusively for peaceful purposes and that the establishment of military bases, installations and fortifications, the testing of any type of weapons and the conduct of military manœuvres on celestial bodies are to be prohibited.

The Treaty does not prohibit the use of military personnel for scientific research or for any other peaceful purposes, or the use of any equipment or facility necessary for the peaceful exploration of the Moon and other celestial bodies.

The Treaty was opened for signature on 27 January 1967 and entered into force on 10 October the same year. As of the end of 1984, 84 States had become parties to the Treaty and another 29 had signed but not yet ratified it.

Preventing an arms race in outer space

The desire of the international community to prevent an arms race in outer space was clearly expressed in the 1978 Final Document, which stated that in order to achieve that objective, further measures should be taken and appropriate negotiations held in accordance with the spirit of the 1967 outer space Treaty (paragraph 80). In fact, a further instrument, the Agreement Governing the Activities of States on the Moon and Other Celestial Bodies, was concluded in 1979. That Agreement, for which the Secretary-General of the United Nations was designated depositary, entered into force on 11 July 1984, upon deposit of the fifth instrument of ratification. It states, *inter alia*, that the Moon and other celestial bodies within the solar system shall be used exclusively for peaceful purposes.

Also in 1979, Italy submitted a memorandum to the Committee on Disarmament in which it called for an additional protocol to the 1967 outer space Treaty to supplement and amplify its legal provisions. In particular, Italy proposed the ban of any action of a military or other hostile nature in outer space, including the launching into orbit or beyond of any devices for offensive purposes, the testing of any weapons or the carrying out of military manœuvres. Such a protocol would not affect, in its opinion, the use of reconnaissance and communication satellites, which also play an important role in verifying disarmament and arms control agreements. It would be intended, however, to prohibit "hunter-killer" satellites designed to interfere with the operation of satellites of other States.

While the question of the peaceful uses of outer space was being discussed in the United Nations, the USSR and the United States commenced parallel bilateral discussions on their anti-satellite activities, following a United States proposal in March 1977 that the two form a joint group to discuss the questions. The first meeting of the Group took place in June 1978 at Helsinki, and the last of a series of three, in June 1979. The talks were suspended that year without the two countries having reached agreement on the issue.

Two years later, in 1981, at the request of the Soviet Union, an item entitled "Conclusion of a treaty on the prohibition of the stationing of weapons of any kind in outer space" was placed on the agenda of the General Assembly. That request was accompanied by a draft treaty. In the First Committee, the Soviet proposal was supported by a number of socialist countries, and Mongolia introduced a draft resolution on the issue by which the Assembly, taking into account the draft treaty, would request the Committee on Disarmament to start negotiations on the text of a treaty to prevent the extension of the arms race into outer space. Also in 1981, Italy, on behalf of a group of Western countries, introduced a draft resolution entitled "Prevention of an arms race in outer space", by which the Assembly was asked to call on all States, particularly those with major space capabilities, to contribute actively to the goal of preventing an arms race in outer space. The Assembly would also request the Committee on Disarmament to consider the question of negotiating effective and verifiable agreements aimed at preventing an arms race in outer space and to give priority attention to the negotiation of an effective and verifiable agreement prohibiting anti-satellite systems. Both resolutions were adopted. Again in 1982, the same two approaches were reflected in two further resolutions. While all four resolutions were supported by large majorities, the Western States generally abstained with regard to the Soviet approach and the socialist countries abstained with regard to the Western initiative.

In addition, in 1982, the question of preventing an arms race in outer space was raised among the subjects of discussion at the Second United Nations Conference on the Exploration and Peaceful Uses of Outer Space, held in Vienna in August.

In 1983 and 1984, at the initiative of Egypt and Sri Lanka, supported by other non-aligned countries, the General Assembly adopted only one resolution by which it requested the Conference on Disarmament to intensify its consideration of the question of the prevention of an arms race in outer space in all its aspects and to establish an *ad hoc* working group with a view to undertaking negotiations for the conclusion of an agreement on that issue. Draft resolutions with alternative approaches were put forward both years but were withdrawn after consultations, without being put to a vote. The single resolution, while still failing to achieve consensus, was widely supported. Thus, in 1983 the resolution was adopted by a vote of 147 to 1 (United States), with 1 abstention (United Kingdom), and in 1984, by a vote of 150 to none, with 1 abstention (United States).

In 1983, under the agenda item requested by the Soviet Union, Mongolia submitted a draft resolution entitled "Conclusion of a treaty on the prohibition of the use of force in outer space and from space against the Earth". In this connection, many socialist States, for example, Mongolia, expressed their appreciation of the unilateral moratorium on launching anti-satellite weapons into outer space which the Soviet Union had assumed. The aim of the draft resolution was a complete ban on the testing and deployment in space of any space-based weapon for the destruction of objects on Earth, in the atmosphere and in outer space. Furthermore, the draft text provided for an unconditional pledge not to create new anti-satellite systems and to destroy those already in existence.

Since 1982, the item on the prevention of an arms race in outer space has also been on the agenda of the Conference on Disarmament. Proposals for the establishment of an *ad hoc* working body have also been considered, though no consensus on an appropriate mandate had been reached as of the end of 1984. The group of 21, the socialist States and China have repeatedly called for initiating negotiations, in a subsidiary body, with a view to concluding an agreement for the prevention of an arms race in outer space, including the questions of space-based weapons and anti-satellite systems. Several Western countries have expressed themselves, in principle, in favour of establishing a subsidiary body to consider the issue. The United States and the United Kingdom, in particular, have long felt that the Conference should first define the mandate of a subsidiary body and then establish it. Late in March 1985, the Conference on Disarmament was able to achieve consensus on the establishment of an *ad hoc* committee on the prevention of an arms race in outer space with a mandate "to examine, as a first step at this stage, through substantive and general consideration, issues relevant to the prevention of an arms race in outer space". Under this arrangement, the Conference will continue its work on the matter.

Proposal for an international satellite
monitoring agency

An initiative relating to outer space was taken by France at the first special session of the General Assembly devoted to disarmament, in 1978. Following the French proposal concerning an international satellite monitoring agency to contribute to the control and verification of international arms regulation and disarmament agreements, the General Assembly requested a study on the subject. That led to the examination and presentation of two reports on the subject by an international group of experts. The first was submitted to the General Assembly in 1979, and it contained preliminary conclusions on the technical, legal and financial implications of establishing such an agency. The second, submitted in 1981 to the Preparatory Committee for the Second Special Session of the General Assembly Devoted to Disarmament, contained an in-depth study on the matter. The latter report, entitled *The Implications of Establishing an International Satellite Monitoring Agency (ISMA)*, subsequently conveyed to the General Assembly at its 1982 special session, was referred to the Assembly at its following regular session for further consideration.

The experts concluded that an ISMA could make a valuable contribution to the verification of disarmament agreements and the prevention or settlement of some international crises. In their opinion, no prohibition existed in international law for carrying out such monitoring activities, and they were also deemed to be technically feasible. While the financial implications of an ISMA appeared to be substantial, a complete system would cost the international community each year well under 1 per cent of annual world-wide military expenditures.

In 1982, also at the initiative of France, the General Assembly at its regular session adopted a resolution by which it reaffirmed the essential role of appropriate monitoring measures in establishing and implementing disarmament agreements and in strengthening international peace and security and requested the Secretary-General to report to it at its next session on the practical modalities for implementing the study's conclusions with respect to the institutional aspects of an ISMA. China, France and the United Kingdom voted for the resolution; the Soviet Union against and the United States abstained. In the explanation of the vote, the Soviet Union pointed out that it voted against because the agency represented an attempt to establish a monitoring or control procedure without any link to actual disarmament measures. Furthermore, in its opinion, no answer was given as to the legal nature of the agency and as to its relationship with existing agreements.

Pursuant to the resolution, the Secretary-General submitted in October 1983 a report on the issue, in which he stated that the General

Assembly would have to decide upon a process and legal framework which could result in the establishment of an ISMA. Should it decide to initiate such a process, it could also identify, according to that report, the specific terms of the responsibilities of the Secretary-General in the framework of the negotiations between the participating States. As of 1984, no further progress had been made on the matter.

Chapter X

Environmental modification techniques

Concern over the general issue of environmental protection from the international standpoint was expressed in the Declaration of the United Nations Conference on the Human Environment, held in Stockholm in 1972. The United Nations Conference maintained that nations were responsible for ensuring that their own activities did not damage the environment of other nations. In 1974, Sweden suggested that the CCD look into possible measures to prevent the use of changes in meteorological patterns that could have military applications.

The importance of the problem stemmed from the fact that scientific and technical progress was not only opening the possibility of influencing the natural environment in beneficial ways – for instance, by artificially induced rainfall, prevention of hailstorms, fog dispersion, neutralization of the destructive force of hurricanes and typhoons – but was also making it possible to use environmental modification techniques for military or other hostile purposes.

These possibilities led to efforts to achieve an international convention prohibiting the artificial modification of the environment for military and other hostile uses even before the techniques involved had become fully developed by States. An acknowledgement of the significance of the issue was indicated when the question of environmental warfare was examined by the Soviet Union and the United States at the summit meeting they held in Moscow in July 1974. In a joint communiqué, the leaders of the two major Powers advocated effective measures to overcome the danger of the use of environmental modification techniques for military purposes.

Also in 1974, at the request of the Soviet Union, an item entitled "Prohibition of action to influence the environment and climate for military and other purposes incompatible with the maintenance of international security, human well-being and health" was placed on the agenda of the General Assembly. In addition, the USSR submitted a draft resolution on the item to which the text of a convention was annexed. The Assembly took note of the draft convention and requested the CCD to proceed as soon as possible towards achieving an agreement on the text of such a convention.

During its 1975 summer session, at the request of Sweden, the CCD held informal meetings on the subject with the participation of experts from 10 countries. The major part of the discussion was devoted to the consideration of various techniques of weather and climate modification and the possible danger of their military application. After the discussions within the negotiating body, the Soviet Union and the United States submitted identical, agreed texts of a nine-article draft convention to the CCD on 21 August 1975.

The preamble of the draft convention, *inter alia*, expressed the realization of States parties that the military use of environmental modification techniques could have effects harmful to human welfare. It also expressed their desire to limit the potential danger to mankind from means of warfare involving the use of environmental modification techniques. Article I of the draft convention prohibited military or any other hostile use of environmental modification techniques having widespread, long-lasting or severe effects, as the means of destruction, damage or injury to another State party. Article II contained a definition of the term "environmental modification techniques" for the purposes of the prohibition contained in article I as well as some examples thereof. Article III provided that the provisions of the convention should not hinder the use of environmental modification techniques for peaceful purposes. In addition, according to article IV, the States parties would undertake to take, in accordance with their constitutional processes, any necessary measures to prohibit and prevent any activity in violation of the provisions of the convention anywhere under its jurisdiction or control, article V of the draft convention included undertakings for consultation and co-operation in solving any problems which might arise in the application of the convention and also made provision for the submission of complaints to the United Nations Security Council. Articles VI through IX contained provisions covering such matters as amendments, duration, entry into force and deposit.

In introducing the draft convention, the USSR and the United States expressed their wish to see it serve as a basis for negotiations in the CCD and stressed their hope that the discussion would lead to early agreement on an international convention. Various delegations, while supporting the concept of a ban on environmental warfare, suggested various modifications in the proposed draft convention.

In particular, Argentina and Mexico were of the view that the convention should provide a comprehensive prohibition, and therefore called for the deletion of the phrase "having widespread, long-lasting or severe effects". In their opinion, that phrase had the effect of legitimizing the use of techniques under the threshold envisaged. Many Western countries favoured retaining the phrase, but believed that there should be some definition of the terms used in it, perhaps in an annex to the convention. Both the United States and the Soviet Union held that the phrase was necessary. The United States emphasized that the implementation and verification of the ban required it. The USSR maintained that it was the best possible presentation consistent with the overall scope of the treaty.

In 1976, the CCD established a working group for the purpose of considering modifications that delegations might wish to propose. The text was accordingly revised, but both the USSR and the United States were confident that the amended draft treaty would still accomplish the main objective of effectively eliminating the real dangers of military or any other hostile use of environmental modification techniques.

As a result, on 18 May 1977, the Convention on the Prohibition of Military or Any Other Hostile Use of Environmental Modification Techniques (ENMOD Convention) was opened for signature in Geneva. It was the first multilateral agreement in the field of arms limitation and disarmament that entrusted depositary functions to the Secretary-General of the United Nations.

Under its basic provision (article I), each State party undertakes not to engage in "military or any other hostile use of environmental modification techniques having widespread, long-lasting or severe effects as the means of destruction, damage or injury to any other State Party".

The term "environmental modification techniques" is defined (article II) as "any technique for changing through the deliberate manipulation of natural processes — the dynamics, composition or structure of the earth, including its biota, lithosphere, hydrosphere and atmosphere, or of outer space".

States parties also agree to facilitate the exchange of information on peaceful use of environmental modification techniques, and to co-operate in the preservation, improvement and peaceful utilization of the environment (article III).

It was the CCD's understanding that the term "widespread" would encompass an area on the scale of several hundred square kilometres; "long-lasting" should be interpreted as lasting for a period of months, or approximately a season; and "severe" should involve serious or significant disruption or harm to human life, natural and economic resources or other national assets.

Another understanding referred to examples of phenomena that could be caused by environmental modification techniques such as earthquakes, tidal waves, upsets in the ecological balance of a region, changes in weather patterns (clouds, precipitation, cyclones and tornadoes) and changes in climate patterns, ocean currents, the ozone layer and the state of the ionosphere. All such phenomena that could reasonably be expected to result in widespread, long-lasting or severe destruction, damage or injury to another State party would therefore be prohibited.

The Convention, after ratification by 20 countries, entered into force on 5 October 1978. As of the end of 1984, there were 47 States parties and 19 States signatories.

The issue of environmental modification techniques was considered at the first special session of the General Assembly devoted to disarmament, in 1978. The General Assembly stated in the Final Document that the Committee on Disarmament should keep under review the need for further prohibition of military or any other hostile use of such modification techniques in order to eliminate the danger to mankind of their use. Thus, in 1979, the Committee agreed that the question would be considered, among others, under the heading "collateral measures" of its permanent agenda.

The question came again to the attention of the General Assembly in 1982, in connection with the preparation and convening of the First Review Conference of the parties to the Convention. According to article VIII, five years after the entry into force of the Convention, a conference would be convened in Geneva in order to review the operation of the Convention with a view to ensuring that its purposes and provisions were being realized.

In pursuance of article VIII of the Convention, a review conference of the States parties to the Convention was held at Geneva from 10 to 20 September 1984. In its Final Declaration, the States parties to the Convention reaffirmed their strong common interest in preventing the use of environmental modification techniques for military or any other hostile purposes. They reaffirmed their strong support for the Convention, their continued dedication to its principles and objectives and their commitment to implement effectively its provisions. The review undertaken by the Conference confirmed that the obligations assumed under article I had been faithfully observed by the States parties. The Conference also expressed the conviction that, taking into account the relevant understandings and the present state of technology, the provisions of that article remained effective in preventing the dangers of military or any other hostile use of environmental modification techniques.

At the same time, the Conference recognized the need to keep under continuing review and examination the provisions of article I, in order to ensure their continued effectiveness, taking into account any developments which might take place in the relevant technology, and having regard to the different views expressed in the course of the debate on that article on the question of expanding its scope.

Chapter XI

Conventional weapons

The question of the regulation and reduction of conventional armaments and armed forces has been taken up by the United Nations concurrently with the question of nuclear weapons and atomic energy almost since the very first session of the General Assembly, in 1946. It has been discussed in various United Nations bodies against a background of concern over rising military expenditures, recognition that general and complete disarmament involves both nuclear and non-nuclear weapons, and awareness of the potentially destabilizing effects at the regional level of increasing arsenals or introducing of new weapons. While effective measures of nuclear disarmament and the prevention of nuclear war have the "highest priority" on the agenda of disarmament negotiating bodies, increasing attention has been given in recent years to the conventional arms race and to disarmament measures relating to conventional weapons and armed forces.

The Final Document of the Assembly's first special session devoted to disarmament stated that "together with negotiations on nuclear disarmament measures, negotiations should be carried out on the balanced reduction of armed forces and of conventional armaments". It further stated that those "negotiations should be conducted with particular emphasis on armed forces and conventional weapons of nuclear-weapon States and other militarily significant countries" (paragraph 22). The Document also made clear that States with the largest military arsenals have a special responsibility in pursuing the process of conventional armaments reductions, and that there should also be negotiations on the limitation of the international transfer of conventional weapons. The Document added that the adoption of those disarmament measures should take place in such an equitable and balanced manner as to ensure the right of each State to undiminished security at any stage until the lowest possible level of armaments and military forces is reached.

In 1980, at the initiative of Denmark, the General Assembly approved in principle the carrying out of a study on all aspects of the conventional arms race and asked the Disarmament Commission to work out the general approach to it, including structure and scope, at its 1981 session. The initiative was adopted, but not by consensus. Some non-aligned and Eastern European States feared that the initiation of the study on this question might distract attention from the priority question of nuclear disarmament. In 1981, however, the Assembly decided on the establishment of a group of qualified experts on the matter, which would pursue its work as soon as the Disarmament Commission had completed the guidelines.

The report, completed in 1984 and entitled *Study on Conventional Disarmament*, discussed for the first time in a United Nations context the nature, causes and effects of the conventional arms race, while addressing principles, approaches and measures for conventional arms limitation and disarmament.

According to the study, the conventional arms race endangers international security by heightening military confrontation and increasing political tensions, thereby raising the possibility of armed conflict between the major Powers. It also threatens to increase the incidence and severity of armed conflicts in different regions of the world and generally impedes the progress of the international community towards a more stable world order.

As a matter of fact, since the end of the Second World War millions of people have been killed by conventional weapons in some 150 conflicts fought in the territories of over 71 States, mostly in the developing areas of the world.

The world's total military expenditure was estimated to be in excess of $800 billion in 1984, with four fifths of that amount being spent on conventional arms and armed forces by major military Powers. If that trend were to persist, it was estimated that it could well reach $1 trillion by 1990. About 70 per cent of expenditures could be attributed to six main military spenders (alphabetically, China, France, Germany, Federal Republic of, USSR, United Kingdom and United States), of which the largest share was by the two major military Powers. That global expenditure on arms and armed forces represented a massive consumption of resources for potentially destructive purposes in contrast to the urgent need for social and economic development for which many of these resources might be used.

Furthermore, the study points out that the world's current armed forces are estimated to total more than 25 million military personnel and that that figure has increased by more than 30 per cent over the previous 20 years. Conservative calculations indicate a total conventional weapons inventory of over 140,000 main battle tanks, over 35,000 combat aircraft, over 21,000 helicopters, over 1,100 major surface warships and over 700 attack submarines.

The study emphasizes the link between technology and the course and pace of the arms race. Technology continually fuels the arms race by making possible the development of new types or new versions of existing types of weapons systems and by creating a climate of uncertainty between rivals about the future. Rapid advances in many areas of science and technology, especially in electronics, telecommunications, computers and directed energy (such as laser beams), have made possible the development of highly complex weapon systems, the study determines. Such advances have pushed conventional warfare towards increased automation. One major trend has been the ongoing development of precision guided munitions (PGMs), not only long-range cruise missiles, but also other weapons with on-board guidance systems, which could fundamentally change the character of conventional warfare.

According to the study, the conventional arms race is closely related to the political tensions and differences between East and West and also to tensions, conflicts and confrontations in other parts of the world. In addition, the conventional arms race generates mistrust and apprehension and is intensified by actions perceived as threatening or hostile.

The study concludes that the problem of the conventional arms race is urgent and requires concrete steps be taken in the field of conventional disarmament. Progress in that direction would to a large extent depend upon the state of relations between the Soviet Union and the United States and States members of the two main alliances. However, there is also a clear possibility for all States to explore what each of them might be able to do in the way of initiating and facilitating efforts aimed at conventional arms limitations and disarmament.

In addition, an enlightened and determined commitment by the public is essential, according to the study, for substantial progress. The role of the United Nations in building such a public commitment would be to provide accurate information and to promote a sound understanding of the issues involved and of the different points of view, as a basis for effective political action for disarmament.

The study notes that progress in curbing the nuclear arms race would facilitate the conventional disarmament effort, by improving relations among the nuclear-weapon States. Furthermore, the States with the largest military arsenals might initiate negotiations aiming at early agreement to not increase their armed forces and conventional armaments, or to reduce them. Agreements should be sought at the global level as well as on a regional or a bilateral basis.

In 1980, when the debate on the broad question of conventional disarmament resulted in the adoption of a resolution which led to the study discussed above, another study, entitled *Study on All the Aspects of Regional Disarmament,* was completed and submitted to the Assembly. It concluded that the "cessation of the conventional arms race is a domain in which the inclusion of a regional aspect in the approach to disarmament is particularly important". (See section on regional disarmament below.)

On the general question of conventional disarmament, differences still persist among Members of the United Nations. While the main proponents of conventional disarmament, such as several Western States and

China, have called for emphasis on both conventional and nuclear disarmament and for the two to be sought simultaneously, many countries, largely non-aligned, continue to caution against equating conventional disarmament with nuclear disarmament. The latter maintain that the greatest threat to mankind is posed by nuclear weapons and that, therefore, nuclear disarmament must remain the highest priority item in all multilateral disarmament efforts, as stated in the 1978 Final Document. Eastern European States express support for substantial reductions of the current levels of conventional armaments and armed forces and have suggested that, as a first step, agreement could be reached not to increase existing arsenals while negotiations on their subsequent reduction are pursued.

Weapons having excessively inhumane or indiscriminate effects

Attempts to stop the use of certain types of weapons considered to be too cruel in their effects began long before the creation of the United Nations and have continued in the name of the laws of humanity.

The St. Petersburg Declaration of 1868 stated that nations should not use weapons which aggravate the suffering of the disabled. When the "dumdum" bullet (which expands or flattens more easily than other bullets, causing more serious wounds) was developed a few years later, it was viewed as contrary to the 1868 Declaration, and participants in the 1899 Hague Conference prohibited its use. The Hague Conferences of 1899 and 1907 also prohibited the use of poison or poisoned weapons, projectiles for diffusion of asphyxiating or deleterious gases, and the discharge of projectiles and explosives from balloons, and restricted the use of underwater contact mines. The Geneva Protocol of 1925, discussed in chapter VIII, renewed the ban on the use of poisonous gases and prohibited the use of analogous materials and bacteriological methods of warfare. Nor is the interest of the United Nations in such matters recent.

Already in 1972, the United Nations expert report *Napalm and Other Incendiary Weapons and All Aspects of Their Possible Use* found that that category of weapons was being used more and more in modern warfare, with increasingly cruel and destructive effects. The Group of Experts appointed by the Secretary-General to prepare the report found that, except for nuclear weapons and certain chemical and biological weapons, "no other armament places such destructive power in the hands of military commanders". The report described the agents and weapons and how they had been used on the battlefield, against urban centres and in rural areas. It explained the painful and terrible effects of incendiaries on the human body, as well as the problems of treatment, and appealed for effective measures for the prohibition of the development, production, stockpiling and use of napalm and other incendiary weapons.

132

After considering the report, the General Assembly deplored the use of such weapons in all armed conflicts and requested the Secretary-General to circulate the report to all Governments for their comments. In 1973 it decided to broaden the consideration of the question to include all other conventional weapons deemed to cause unnecessary suffering or to have indiscriminate effects, and to seek agreement on rules prohibiting or restricting the use of such weapons. Thus, it adopted a resolution on that question by a recorded vote of 103 to none with 18 abstentions.

A later study by experts convened under the auspices of the International Committee of the Red Cross, entitled *Weapons That May Cause Unnecessary Suffering or Have Indiscriminate Effects*, concluded that all incendiary weapons, as well as a number of other specific conventional weapons, tended to cause excessive suffering or to have indiscriminate effects, and should therefore be prohibited. The question of banning such weapons was also among matters considered by the Diplomatic Conference on the Reaffirmation and Development of International Humanitarian Law Applicable in Armed Conflicts, held at Geneva in several sessions from 1974 to 1977.

In order to carry on the useful work which had been accomplished by the Diplomatic Conference, the Assembly decided in 1977 to convene a United Nations conference on excessively injurious conventional weapons, stating its conviction that the suffering of civilian populations and combatants could be significantly reduced if general agreement could be attained to prohibit or restrict their use. Moreover, the Assembly stated, positive results in that area would serve as encouragement in the broader field of disarmament, and could lead to steps to eliminate the categories of weapons whose use was banned. Thus the first major international conference on the prohibition or restriction of specific conventional weapons since the Hague Conferences was convened by the United Nations in Geneva in September 1979.

Proposals submitted to the Conference concerned the prohibition or restriction of napalm and other incendiary weapons, blast weapons relying on shock waves caused by the detonation of substances spread in the air and fuel-air explosives; anti-personnel cluster warheads or other devices with many bomblets which eject a great number of small fragments or which release projectiles in the form of flechettes or needles; mines and booby traps; and new types of small-calibre projectiles or bullets whose effects were said to be comparable to those of the dumdum bullet.

The Conference focused on the drafting of three protocols, one concerning non-detectable fragments, another concerning land-mines and booby traps and a third concerning incendiary weapons, and on a general, "umbrella" treaty to serve as the framework for the protocols concerning the specific categories of weapons.

In 1980, the Conference concluded its work, adopting unanimously the following instruments: Convention on Prohibitions or Restrictions on the Use of Certain Conventional Weapons Which May Be Deemed to Be Excessively Injurious or to Have Indiscriminate Effects; Protocol on Non-Detectable Fragments (Protocol I); Protocol on Prohibitions or Restrictions on the Use of Mines, Booby-traps and Other Devices (Protocol II); Protocol on Prohibitions or Restrictions on the Use of Incendiary Weapons (Protocol III); and Resolution on Small-Calibre Weapons Systems. The Convention is an "umbrella" treaty under which additional specific agreements can be concluded in the form of protocols.

The Convention and the Protocols provide new rules for the protection of civilians and civilian objects and, in some cases, also military personnel. Protocol I prohibits the use of any weapon whose primary effect is to injure by fragments which in the human body escape detection by X-rays. Protocol II and a technical annex to it relate to the use on land of the mines, booby traps and other devices defined therein, such as those activated by remote control or automatically after a lapse of time, including mines laid to interdict beaches, waterway crossings and river crossings, but do not apply to the use of anti-ship mines. Protocol III prohibits in all circumstances the making of the civilian population as such the object of attack by incendiary weapons, and restricts their use against military objectives. "Incendiary weapon" is intended to be any weapon or munition which is primarily designed to set fire to objects or to cause burn injury to persons through the action of flame, heat, or a combination thereof, produced by a chemical reaction of a substance delivered on the target. The rules range from a complete ban on the use of such weapons to restrictions on their indiscriminate use against civilians or civilian objects. While the rules embodied in the Convention and Protocols do not go as far as many countries had hoped, they are a significant step in the development of humanitarian laws intended to protect civilians and to reduce the suffering of victims of armed conflict.

The Secretary-General of the United Nations, who was designated the depositary of the Convention, opened it for signature at Headquarters in New York on 10 April 1981. The Convention entered into force on 2 December 1983. By the end of 1984, the Convention had been ratified by 24 countries, while 31 other States had signed it.

The regional approach

As already stated, the possibility of regional approaches to disarmament has received considerable attention in recent years. Regional arms limitation has been viewed as one way to contribute towards general and complete disarmament on a global basis. The 1980 *Study on All the Aspects of Regional Disarmament* was the result of an initiative of Belgium. The Group of Experts which prepared it found that most States perceived threats to their security and their need for military preparedness as primarily related to conditions in their own region. The study makes clear, however, that progress in disarmament and avoidance of deterioration of political and security conditions at the global level would greatly facilitate agreement on regional measures. Equally, progress in disarmament and the equitable solution of problems at the regional level would promote relaxation of tension and disarmament at the global level and help keep regions free of external interference and rivalry. According to the study, in order to facilitate the success of regional arrangements, extraregional States should respect security-enhancing measures agreed upon in the regional context.

The study reviews past experiences and current endeavours such as: the establishment of zones free of nuclear weapons in Antarctica and Latin America, including the proposals for nuclear-weapon-free zones in various regions of the world, the Vienna Talks on Mutual Reduction of Forces and Armaments and Associated Measures in Central Europe and the efforts within the framework of the Conference on Security and Co-operation in Europe and its follow-up. In addition, the study suggests measures that could be applied in a regional context relating, *inter alia*, to nuclear weapons, conventional weapons, military expenditures, the relaxation of international tensions, prevention of the use of force and promotion of public opinion in favour of disarmament.

The experts conclude that while the ultimate goals of disarmament are fundamentally the same for all countries, namely, to attain genuine security, to avert the danger of war and to release additional resources for peaceful ends, conditions between regions differ to such an extent that acceptable first steps could not be the same in all of them. First steps in some cases might focus on the peaceful resolution of disputes, in others on the reduction of forces with a view to establishing or maintaining an equitable force relationship and in still others on non-involvement in confrontations between extraregional Powers or the avoidance of external interference.

One particular merit of the regional approach, according to the study, is the possibility of taking advantage of such differences. It therefore recognizes the need for analyses of possible disarmament steps region by region, conducted in the light of the security situation and political conditions of the region. To that end, the study sees a need for regional mechanisms or institutions which would allow development of initiatives and negotiation of concrete steps.

In 1982, the Assembly adopted unanimously a resolution on regional disarmament by which, *inter alia*, it expressed the hope that Governments would consult with each other on appropriate regional disarmament measures which could be taken at the initiative and with the participation of all the States concerned and called on the Department for Disarmament Affairs and UNIDIR to lend assistance to States and regional institutions which might request it in such a context. The following year, in 1983, the Assembly adopted a similar resolution in which it expressed its satisfaction at the convening in Stockholm early in 1984 of the Conference on Confidence- and Security-building Measures and Disarmament in Europe. The resolution also requested the Secretary-General to keep the General Assembly regularly informed on the implementation of the resolution adopted the previous year as well as of the activities carried out by the Secretariat and UNIDIR in the field of the regional approach to disarmament. In 1984, the General Assembly requested a further report on those activities.

In addition to more general considerations of conventional weapons, over the years, a number of specific efforts have been made in this regard in the context of different regions.

DECLARATION OF AYACUCHO

On 9 December 1974, Argentina, Bolivia, Chile, Colombia, Ecuador, Panama, Peru and Venezuela adopted at Lima a declaration in which they expressed their commitment to create conditions conducive to effective arms limitation and to stop the acquisition of arms for aggressive ends. They also condemned the use of nuclear energy for other than peaceful purposes. At the request of the above-mentioned States, the text of the Declaration was conveyed to the United Nations early in 1975.

The principles of the Declaration were reaffirmed in 1978 in a joint communiqué issued by the foreign ministers of the same countries, in which they expressed their countries' willingness to explore, together with the other Latin American countries, possibilities for reaching an agreement on limiting conventional weapons in the region.

Subsequently, at a meeting in Mexico City in August 1978, representatives from 20 Latin American and Caribbean countries agreed to propose for the consideration of their Governments the establishment of a regional consultative mechanism relating to disarmament matters in the field of conventional weapons in general, and called upon all countries of the region to participate in those endeavours.

Activities since that time, however, have not brought about conclusive results.

MUTUAL REDUCTION OF FORCES AND ARMAMENTS AND ASSOCIATED MEASURES IN CENTRAL EUROPE

Negotiations on the mutual reduction of forces and armaments and associated measures in Central Europe first opened in Vienna on 30 October 1973 and since then have constituted an important regional effort. The NATO and Warsaw Treaty States participating in the negotiations are Belgium, Canada, Czechoslovakia, the German Democratic Republic, the Federal Republic of Germany, Luxembourg, the Netherlands,

Poland, the Soviet Union, the United Kingdom and the United States. Furthermore, Bulgaria, Denmark, Greece, Hungary, Italy, Norway, Romania and Turkey participate with special status. The United Nations is not officially informed of the negotiating process. However, the States participating in the negotiations and other Member States have, since 1972, frequently referred to the importance of these talks at various sessions of the General Assembly, expressing their hope that they would lead to the solution of the issues under discussion.

The goal, as stated jointly by the participating States in a communiqué dated 28 June 1973, is to contribute to a more stable relationship and to the strengthening of peace and security in Europe, while maintaining undiminished security for each party. However, the positions of the two sides as to practical ways of reaching this goal have differed in important respects.

Western participants have maintained that there is a considerable disparity of forces in terms of manpower and equipment which, together with geography, favours the Eastern side. Any agreement on the reduction and limitation of forces designed to achieve a more stable relationship should therefore, in their view, provide for the elimination of the existing imbalance by implementing adequate reductions which should not necessarily be the same for both sides.

In contrast, Eastern participants have maintained that there is approximate equality between the forces of the two sides and that, consequently, the reduction of armed forces, along with their combat equipment, by equal percentages or the reduction in numbers on the basis of an equitable mutually agreed solution would be the most appropriate way of preserving the existing equilibrium, but at a lower level of forces. The importance of reducing armaments, including nuclear weapons within the area, has also been stressed by Eastern participants. With regard to the geographical factor, they have felt that it is reflected in the overall equilibrium.

Generally speaking, while there is broad agreement on the ceiling of forces to be deployed (some 900,000 among Belgium, Czechoslovakia, German Democratic Republic, Germany, Federal Republic of, Luxembourg, Netherlands and Poland), differences still persist between the two sides with respect to the numbers currently stationed in the area. In addition, there have been disagreements on how to verify the withdrawals.

CONFIDENCE-BUILDING MEASURES

According to the Final Document of the 1978 first special session of the General Assembly devoted to disarmament, in order to facilitate the process of disarmament, it is necessary to take measures and pursue policies to strengthen international peace and security and to build confidence among States. The Final Document refers specifically to the need "to strengthen institutions for maintaining peace and the settlement of international disputes by peaceful means". The General Assembly has subsequently adopted various resolutions on confidence-building measures, and the study entitled *Comprehensive Study on Confidence-building Measures* was prepared by the Secretary-General on these issues in 1981 at the initiative of the Federal Republic of Germany. The Disarmament Commission, furthermore, has been working recently on a set of guidelines for appropriate types of confidence-building measures. Yet, because of differences of approach, particularly between large-scale political means and concrete military measures, towards building confidence, no consensus has been reached so far.

The issue of confidence- and security-building measures has also been discussed within the framework of the Conference on Security and Co-operation in Europe (CSCE). The Conference, in which 33 European countries, Canada and the United States took part, was a non-United Nations forum held in several sessions in Geneva and Helsinki from 3 July 1972 to 1 August 1975. The Conference adopted in Helsinki its Final Act, which included provisions related to security, human rights and economic and scientific co-operation. Major follow-up Conferences to review progress in the implementation of the Helsinki Final Act were held first in Belgrade, from 1977 to 1978, and then in Madrid, from 1980 to 1983.

After reviewing numerous proposals and making considerable compromises, the Madrid Conference agreed to convene a complementary conference, as part of the follow-up process. Consequently, the Conference on Confidence- and Security-building Measures and Disarmament in Europe (CDE) opened in January 1984 in Stockholm. The aim of the Conference is to undertake, in stages, new, effective and concrete actions designed to make progress in strengthening confidence and security and in subsequently achieving lower levels of armaments in Europe. The first stage is expected to last until 1986 (when the CDE will report to the CSCE in Vienna) and is devoted to the negotiation and adoption of confidence- and security-building measures to cover all of Europe, as well as the adjoining sea areas from the Atlantic to the Urals.

Arms transfers

Although not at the centre of conventional disarmament problems, arms transfers represent an important element of the phenomenon of the global arms race and take place in a wide range of contexts, extending from normal trade to outright gifts. According to the 1984 SIPRI *Yearbook*, over the period from 1979 to 1983, the volume of major weapons delivered ceased to grow, primarily because of the world economic recession. However, compared with the previous five-year period, the total volume of such transfers was still about 30 per cent greater, measured in constant United States dollars.

In 1972 the world total arms transfers stood at $20.3 billion measured in constant 1981 values. In 1982 the total was estimated to be $34.3 billion. As also mentioned in the report of the United Nations on conventional disarmament, during the five-year period from 1978 to 1982, the Soviet Union and the United States accounted for about a third each of total arms exports of major weapons. The largest group of importers of major weapons comprises the industrialized countries themselves, whose imports totalled almost as much as the countries of Latin America, Africa and Asia combined. The largest single region importing major weapons has been the Middle East.

It is to be noted that in the same period as much as 90 per cent of all arms transfers stemmed from a group of only six countries (alphabetically, France, Germany, Federal Republic of, Italy, USSR, United Kingdom and United States). Arms transfers have important economic and commercial aspects. They may serve to improve the balance of payment position of the supplier country *vis-à-vis* major recipients. They may also contribute to the competitive efforts of segments of the arms industry to maintain a technological lead and achieve a growing share of the market world-wide. One of the trends of arms transfers in recent years has been the shift in sales from surplus or outdated weapons systems to advanced and up-to-date weapons systems which often require specialized training and maintenance work. This often involves the presence in the recipient country of instructors and technical personnel for protracted periods of time, which further increases the degree of dependence on the supplier country.

The question of arms transfers was first considered separately by the General Assembly in 1965, when Malta proposed a system that could give publicity to all arms transfers. Lacking the support of the majority of Member States, its proposal was not accepted. In 1968, Denmark, together with other countries, proposed that the General Assembly seek the views of Governments on the idea of developing a United Nations register of the trade in arms. Again the proposal was unable to generate wide support and was not pressed to a vote.

It was eight years later, in 1976, that Japan initiated a proposal whereby the General Assembly would call for views of States and a factual study on weapons transfers. A procedural action by some non-aligned States prevented the proposal from being put to a vote. A further proposal for the publication by the United Nations of data on the production and transfer of weapons systems was placed before the CCD by Italy in 1977. The Italian proposal envisaged the establishment of a commission and regional subcommissions, in which the main arms suppliers would take part, with the aim of maintaining conventional armaments at their lowest possible level consistent with the security of States.

In 1977, the United States took a unilateral approach by accepting restraints on arms supplies, under certain specified conditions, while promoting co-operation between supplier and recipient nations and encouraging regional co-operation among the latter. Because of the absence of similar actions by other supplier countries, the United States declared the following year that the unilateral approach, if it had to remain such, was ineffective. Also in 1977 and 1978, the Soviet Union and the United States carried out bilateral talks on conventional arms transfers with the goal of curtailing the volume of armaments transferred by the two major suppliers: the talks did not lead to any results.

Attempts to have resolutions adopted on arms transfers have not been successful so far. While there is general concern at the transfer of conventional weapons, the position held mostly by non-aligned countries is that any restraint on arms transfers without restraint on arms production would operate against recipient countries needing weapons to defend their independence and territorial integrity, and that priority attention should be devoted to nuclear disarmament and the central arms race between the two major nuclear-weapon States and their allies.

In 1978, in the Final Document of the first special session on disarmament, adopted by consensus, it was stated that consultations should be carried out among major arms suppliers and recipient countries on the limitation of all types of international transfer of conventional weapons.

While the regional approach has been widely supported by countries of all geographical, political and economic backgrounds, it is mainly Western developed countries that have stressed its value in the pursuit of conventional disarmament. Non-aligned countries have generally emphasized the need to take into account the special characteristics and security situations existing in the respective regions. They have also argued that the conventional arms race, particularly in its international transfer aspect, has gone far beyond local or regional levels and that, therefore, effective efforts against it must involve both supplier and recipient countries and be pursued at broader multilateral levels.

According to the 1984 *Study on Conventional Disarmament*, already mentioned, for any proposed measure concerning arms transfers to receive serious consideration several concerns must be met. All countries have to be satisfied that the proposals are not discriminatory; consultations should be based in particular on the principle of undiminished security of the parties with a view to promoting or enhancing stability at a lower military level; and concerns about the sufficiency of data on arms production and transfers and about the security aspects of providing such information would have to be properly addressed. Furthermore, agreements to restrain the transfer of arms would have to give particular attention to weapons systems whose characteristics are perceived as threatening to the security of other countries. In addition, the participation of both suppliers and recipients would be necessary in order to ensure that third party supplier countries would not simply increase their share of the market by filling any resultant vacuum in recipient countries. In

140

keeping with this, the latter could negotiate local agreements on arms-import restrictions which would, according to the study, both enhance the security situation in the respective regions and reduce the involvement of extraregional States.

While no specific items on arms transfers have been on the agenda of the Conference on Disarmament or that of the Disarmament Commission, in recent years such matters have been discussed from time to time in the context of other issues in those forums, as well as in the debates in the General Assembly.

Chapter XII
Economic and social consequences of the arms race, disarmament and development

Throughout the history of the United Nations there has been not only an emphasis on benefitting development through disarmament, but also recurrent proposals for a specific institutional link to foster this reallocation of resources from armaments to development. As early as 1955, the establishment of an international fund for development and mutual assistance was proposed by France. The proposed fund was part of a comprehensive and detailed "draft agreement on the financial supervision of disarmament and allocation for peaceful purposes of the funds made available", submitted to the Disarmament Commission in Geneva.

According to this plan, States would agree to reduce their military expenditures by a percentage that would increase from year to year; the resources thus released would be transferred to the fund. The fund authority would be charged with setting up and policing a uniform definition of military expenditures with a standardized nomenclature for military budget items. States party to the agreement would have the obligation of communicating all documents relating to their military expenditures to the fund. This plan represents an early proposal for disarmament through reduction in military budgets.

The draft agreement also envisaged arms limitation agreements which would then be converted into corresponding reductions in military budgets under the supervision of the fund. In this latter case, the monitoring of military budgets by the fund would serve as a means of verification of the agreed disarmament measures. Part of the resources released to the fund through the agreed reductions in military budgets would be left at the disposal of the Government concerned and another part would be made available to the fund to be allocated for development. With a view to problems of conversion, the draft agreement mandated that 75 per cent of the funds thus allocated would be spent in the donor country. In this scheme, budgetary control was seen as a suitable alternative to "material control" of a disarmament agreement by technical or other means.

In March 1956, the Soviet Union proposed that a special fund for assistance to developing countries that would be financed through reductions in military budgets be established within the United Nations. Two years later, the Soviet Union renewed and elaborated that proposal. In a memorandum annexed to a request for the inclusion in the Assembly's agenda of an item concerning the reduction of military budgets, the Soviet Union emphasized that the proposed budgetary approach was part of a "practical method of solving the disarmament problem" by "gradual, partial measures". A draft resolution, which it subsequently submitted to the First Committee, called for a reduction in the military budgets of the USSR, the United States, the United Kingdom and France of 10 to 15 per cent and the use of part of the savings for development assistance.

In 1964, Brazil submitted a working paper to the Eighteen-Nation Committee on Disarmament in Geneva on the application of savings on military expenditures, which called for the establishment of an industrial conversion and economic development fund. The fund would be allotted not less than 20 per cent of the global value of reductions in military budgets which would then be utilized for financing development assistance. The Brazilian working paper emphasized that the economic and social imbalance then prevailing in the world was, because of the social tensions it entailed, a serious threat to international peace and security and that the struggle against misery would encourage the economic development of the world as a whole.

In 1973, the General Assembly adopted, at the initiative of the Soviet Union, a resolution calling for a 10 per cent reduction in the military budgets of States permanent members of the Security Council and the allocation of 10 per cent of the funds thus saved for social and economic development in the developing countries. The resolution also called on other States with major military and economic potential to participate. This was conceived, initially at least, as a one-time reduction in military budgets. A special committee would be set up to distribute the funds, which were to be additional to existing development assistance, without discrimination of any kind. A companion resolution, introduced by Mexico, called for an expert study of the technical and other problems associated with agreements for the reduction of military budgets. The resulting report led to a series of expert studies on problems of measuring, comparing and verifying the military expenditures of States.

A number of new proposals for an institutional link such as a fund between disarmament and development were made at the first special session of the General Assembly devoted to disarmament, in 1978. The President of Senegal, for instance, proposed that a tax on armaments be instituted, based on the military budgets of States. The tax, amounting to 5 per cent of military expenditures and payable to the United Nations, would be used solely for development assistance. Senegal believed that such a tax would raise $20 billion per annum in revenue.

The President of France, for his part, proposed the establishment of an international disarmament fund for development, which would channel funds released by disarmament into development. This proposal, which was subsequently elaborated in a memorandum of the French Government, envisioned the fund as a new United Nations specialized agency, which would constitute a practical manifestation of the relationship acknowledged by the world community to exist between disarmament and development. Contributors to the fund would be those States which were both the most heavily armed and the most developed; beneficiaries of the fund would be those States which were the least heavily armed and the least developed. In principle, the fund would be based on the disarmament-dividend approach, that is, on resources released by disarmament measures. However, the French proposal also provided for a transitional phase with an initial one-time endowment of $1 billion, until the fund could be financed on a long-term basis from resources derived from disarmament savings. In its transitional phase, contributions to the fund would be assessed on the basis of a State's level of armament, measured by the possession of certain types of weapons systems, the existence of which, according to the proposal, could be objectively determined. Both contributor States and potential beneficiary States subscribing to the agreement establishing the fund would be fund members and the principle of balance between the two would be the basis of decision-making. The fund would make grants or loans to developing countries or to intergovernmental organizations, utilizing existing international agencies for the administration of its loans and grants as much as possible. It was further proposed that payments made by contributor States through the fund should be counted towards the United Nations target of 0.7 per cent of GNP for official development assistance.

Mexico, while endorsing the French initiative, proposed the immediate opening of a special *ad hoc* account in the United Nations Development Programme (UNDP) on a provisional basis. Mexico stressed the need to establish practical procedures to channel and distribute to the developing countries a considerable part of the resources that might be released by effective disarmament measures.

Romania, for its part, proposed the freezing and gradual reduction of military budgets on the basis of a concrete programme. In a first stage, the military budgets were to be reduced by at least 10 per cent and one half of the amounts thus released would be transferred unconditionally to a United Nations fund for development, especially for the benefit of countries with a *per capita* income of less than $200.

In May 1984, the parties to the Warsaw Treaty proposed, *inter alia*, negotiations with NATO on the non-increase and reduction of military expenditures in either percentage or absolute terms. The proposal also included the idea of a single, limited, symbolic reduction in military budgets by States of both military alliances on the basis of mutual example. The proposal was conveyed to the 1984 session of the Disarmament Commission, which, while not able to conclude its work on the question, reaffirmed that it was possible to achieve continued and systematic reductions in military expenditures without prejudice to the right of all States to undiminished security, self-defence and sovereignty.

There have also been a number of recent proposals made by non-governmental organizations and individual experts for the creation, in the form of some kind of fund, of an institutional link between disarmament and development. For instance, the report of the Independent Commission on International Development Issues (the Brandt Commission) proposed that consideration be given to the establishment of a world development fund to better meet the financial needs of developing countries and, in particular, to provide new sources of additional and long-term programme funding. The Commission suggested a number of potential new revenue sources which would have the requisite character of automaticity, *inter alia*, the possibility of a tax on military expenditures or a tax on trade in arms. Other suggestions included taxation of international trade in general, international trade in crude oil, energy consumption and durable luxury goods.

The realization that there is a vast misallocation of resources for armaments, which would be better utilized to meet real human needs and, in particular, the urgent requirements of development in the developing countries, underlies all of these proposals. They embody, in various combinations, three approaches for raising contributions for a fund to promote the reallocation of resources from armaments to development:

(*a*) The disarmament-dividend approach, in which the savings resulting from disarmament measures, or a portion thereof, are allocated to development needs;

(*b*) The armaments-levy approach, in which national assessments for contributions to development are based on some agreed measure of States' allocation of resources for military purposes;

(*c*) Voluntary contributions on the model of numerous other United Nations funds and specialized agencies, in which each State determines its own individual contribution.

In 1984, the General Assembly adopted resolution 39/160, by which, *inter alia,* it decided to convene an international conference on the relationship between disarmament and development. The International Conference on the Relationship between Disarmament and Development, to be preceded by thorough preparation, should review the relationship between disarmament and development in all its aspects and dimensions. It should undertake an examination of the implications of the level and magnitude of military expenditures for the world economy and social situation and should make recommendations for remedial measures. The Conference is expected to consider ways and means of releasing additional resources, through disarmament measures, for development purposes, in particular in favour of developing countries. In this connection, the General Assembly also decided to set up a Preparatory Committee for the Conference, composed of 54 Members, which should formulate and submit by consensus at its session in 1985, recommendations as to the provisional agenda, procedure, place, date and duration of the Conference.

United Nations studies and their follow-up

In addition to numerous specific proposals put forward by Member States with a view to promoting economic and social development in conjunction with disarmament efforts, the General Assembly has, over the years and on various occasions, requested the Secretary-General to prepare with the assistance of experts a number of in-depth studies. Their objective has been, on the one hand, to facilitate a better understanding of the problems involved and, on the other, to serve as a basis for decisions on concrete actions, following disarmament measures, to release real resources being used for military purposes for economic and social development, particularly for the benefit of the developing countries. These studies deal with three distinct areas of concern: (*a*) economic and social consequences of the arms race and of military expenditures; (*b*) disarmament and development and (*c*) reduction of military budgets.

A. ECONOMIC AND SOCIAL CONSEQUENCES OF THE ARMS RACE AND OF MILITARY EXPENDITURES

As noted earlier, the first United Nations study on the subject, entitled *Economic and Social Consequences of Disarmament*, was prepared in 1962. It was subsequently updated on two occasions, in 1972 and 1977, under the title *Economic and Social Consequences of the Arms Race and of Military Expenditures*. The latter study concluded, *inter alia*, that as long as the arms race was allowed to continue, it would aggravate world problems of development, economic imbalance and inflation, pollution, scarcity of energy and raw materials, trade relations and technology, while delaying progress in areas such as health, education and housing. Effective disarmament, the study noted, would require reductions in military budgets and curtailment of further developments in weaponry. Particular responsibility for progress in those areas lay with the two largest military Powers, together with other militarily significant States. In addition to that, the study found that the arms race undermined national, regional and international security and increased the risk of both local conflicts and nuclear war.

In 1980, the General Assembly, noting that new developments had occurred since the preparation of the previous studies, requested the Secretary-General to bring them up to date. The updated study, completed in 1982, describes the arms race as a major threat to international security. It also illustrates a triangular relationship between disarmament, security and development.

According to the study, every year global military activities absorb a volume of resources equivalent to as much as two thirds of the gross national product of those countries which together comprise the poorest half of the world's population. The study also estimates that up to 60 million people are engaged in military-related occupations. Military spending, the study further states, not only diverts vast resources away from production and growth within countries, thereby contributing to inflation and economic crises, but also directly and indirectly hinders international exchanges. As a further consequence, international trade is being distorted by political and strategic considerations, thus causing misallocations of resources on a global scale.

In order to prevent resources from being consumed for military ends, the study calls for their conversion to non-military purposes and their diversion to socio-economic development. The redeployment of capital from the military to the civilian sectors of the economy and the similar diversion of military research and development, which could lead to the creation of new technologies for the benefit of the developing countries, are mentioned as important measures in that regard. The study also advocates further exploration of the benefits which would accrue from major measures of disarmament, such as the reduction of military budgets. It states that, until appropriate international agreements are negotiated, self-restraint in the field of military expenditure should be encouraged, and the United Nations, for its part, should intensify its ongoing activities to that end. The reduction of military budgets is also described as a practical step which would permit the transfer of resources from military to civilian use.

The study further notes that increased openness of information about military spending is a necessary condition for public accountability of the socio-economic costs of the arms race.

The General Assembly has adopted a number of resolutions on issues related to the areas covered by the study. In addition, in 1982, it requested the Secretary-General to make the necessary arrangements to publicize the issues within the framework of the activities of the World Disarmament Campaign. The Assembly also decided that matters related to the economic and social consequences of the arms race should be kept under constant review and that an item on the question should be included in the provisional agenda of its fortieth session, in 1985.

B. DISARMAMENT AND DEVELOPMENT

The 1978 Final Document of the first special session of the General Assembly devoted to disarmament reiterated the findings of the first

United Nations study on the relationship between disarmament and development, completed in 1972, which had stated that in a world of finite resources there was a close relationship between expenditure on armaments and economic and social development, and it requested the Secretary-General to initiate a new study.

The study, in which 27 experts participated, was completed in 1981 and represented the first attempt by the United Nations to investigate systematically and in depth the whole range of relationships between balanced and sustainable global economic and social development on the one hand, and disarmament on the other, through the reallocation of some of the resources released by the disarmament process.

Originally proposed by Sweden, the project turned out to be the most comprehensive study in the field of disarmament ever undertaken at the request of the General Assembly. It covered three major areas: (*a*) present utilization of resources for military purposes; (*b*) economic and social effects of a continuing arms race and disarmament measures; and (*c*) conversion and redeployment of resources from military to development purposes. The experts came to the unanimous conclusion that the world could either continue to pursue the arms race or move towards a more sustainable, international economic and political order. It could not do both.

One of the experts' aims was to produce results that could effectively guide the formulation of practical measures to reallocate resources being used for military purposes to civilian pursuits at the local, national, regional and international levels. To that end, *inter alia*, the study analyses the possibilities of conversion of industry from military to civilian purposes and provides a list of possible products that could be manufactured by converted military industrial plants. It suggests that Governments should accordingly undertake the necessary preparations to facilitate the conversion of resources freed by disarmament measures to civilian purposes.

The study also has a number of recommendations to Governments aimed at publicizing the short- and long-term effects of military expenditures and the benefits that would result from reallocating them for economic and social purposes. It suggests, for instance, that Governments systematically compile and disseminate more data on the military use of human and material resources as well as on arms transfers. It also calls for United Nations organs and agencies in their disarmament-related public information and education activities to place increased emphasis on the potential social and economic benefits that could derive from disarmament measures.

In addition, the study recommends that further consideration be given to the idea of establishing an international fund for development and specifically indicates that possible modalities of setting up and administering it should be investigated by the United Nations.

In 1982, the General Assembly adopted a resolution on disarmament and development. By that resolution, among other things, it decided to include in the provisional agenda of its 1985 session the question of the reallocation and conversion of resources through disarmament measures from military to civilian purposes. It also recommended that an investigation regarding the modalities of an international disarmament fund for development be undertaken by UNIDIR in consultation with other relevant international institutions.

Pursuant to a 1983 resolution on the matter, the Disarmament Commission, at its 1984 session, discussed the relationship between disarmament and development. While it was unable to make substantive recommendations on the item, it agreed to include in its report to the General Assembly the main views and proposals put forward. These included, *inter alia*, a French proposal for an international conference on the subject. The Commission recommended that efforts be continued to enable the General Assembly to reach, at its 1984 session, a broad measure of agreement on that subject, taking into account the views contained in its report.

At its session in 1984, the General Assembly decided, on the basis of the report of the Disarmament Commission, to convene an international conference on the relationship between disarmament and development, as proposed by France. The purposes of the Conference would be to review the relationship between disarmament and development in order to reach appropriate conclusions, to undertake an examination of the implications of military expenditures and to consider ways and means to release additional resources, through disarmament measures, for development purposes, in particular in favour of developing countries. The Assembly also decided to set up a preparatory committee, composed of 54 members, which would formulate, by consensus, and submit recommendations on the agenda, procedures, place, date and duration of the Conference to the Assembly at its next session.

C. REDUCTION OF MILITARY BUDGETS

As already pointed out, at the initiative of Mexico, a series of expert studies on the question of the reduction of military budgets began in 1973. The first one, entitled *Reduction of the Military Budgets of States Permanent Members of the Security Council by 10 Per Cent and Utilization of Part of the Funds Thus Saved to Provide Assistance to Developing Countries*, issued in 1974, discussed data relating to military expenditures and development aid and noted that a prerequisite for negotiating reductions in military budgets was agreement on what should and should not be included in those budgets. The difficulties of developing a standardized system of measuring military expenditures and of verifying any agreement to reduce them were also mentioned.

In 1975, the Assembly adopted a resolution, initiated by Mexico and Sweden, by which it urged the two States with the highest military expenditures, the Soviet Union and the United States, to reduce them, and appealed to all States to strive to reach agreement on reductions in their military budgets. It also called for an expert study on the definition and scope of the military sector, as well as on the valuation of resources used by the military sector, allowing for deflation for price changes, international value comparison and other relevant matters. The resultant study, completed in 1976 under the title *Reduction of Military Budgets: Measurement and International Reporting of Military Expenditures*, contained recommendations on the definition and scope of the military sector and expenditures, and presented a reporting formula or matrix as an instrument for the standardized reporting system.

The suggested reporting form called for about 50 items of data under three main ·headings: operating costs, procurement and construction costs, and research and development costs. Each item was to be broken down by types of forces: strategic, general purpose, central support, paramilitary, civil defence and military assistance. The study also suggested that the international reporting instrument be tested and refined by a panel of experienced practitioners in the field of military budgeting. The experts stated that orderly reporting of military expenditures would be the first step towards the "universally desired objective" of reducing military expenditures.

The next stage, called for by the General Assembly, resulted in the 1977 report of an intergovernmental group of budgetary experts which analysed comments of States, considered further development of the reporting system and examined practical problems which budgetary experts would face in completing the recommended format and in extracting appropriate information from the data contributed by States. The report noted that much progress had been made in refining an international reporting format and that the matrix developed provided a good balance between the needs for detail and verifiability and the complexity of reporting in complete detail. One country, Sweden, had tried out the reporting formula with success, and others had indicated that there would not be excessive difficulty in supplying the required expenditure data.

At its 1978 special session devoted to disarmament, the General Assembly stated in its Final Document that the gradual reduction of military budgets on a mutually agreed basis, particularly by the nuclear-weapon States and other militarily significant States, would be a measure that would contribute to the curbing of the arms race and that would increase the possibilities of reallocating resources being used for military purposes to economic and social development (paragraph 89). At its regular session in 1978, the General Assembly requested that a panel of experienced practitioners in the field of military budgeting carry out a practical test of the proposed reporting instrument, with the voluntary co-operation of States from different regions and representing different budgeting and accounting systems. The experts were to assess the results of the test and develop recommendations for further refinement and implementation of the reporting instrument.

The resulting study, entitled *Reduction of Military Budgets: International reporting of military expenditures*, was submitted to the Assembly in 1980 and contained an overview of the replies received from 14 countries. In addition, it provided a qualitative and quantitative analysis of the replies, including computerized tables and suggestions concerning minor modifications of the reporting instrument and the instructions relating to it. Furthermore, the study dealt with problems of comparability of military expenditures and, finally, it presented conclusions, which were generally favourable, as to the viability of the reporting instrument. The experts also recommended that further study be undertaken on the problems of comparison and verification.

In 1982 yet another study, requested by the General Assembly at the initiative of Sweden, entitled *Reduction of Military Budgets: Refinement of International Reporting and Comparison of Military Expenditures*, was prepared by a group of experts. Its aim was to refine further the reporting instrument and examine and suggest solutions to the question of comparing military expenditures under varying budgetary systems, inflation and exchange rates. The experts reaffirmed that the reporting instrument represented a practical means for the regular monitoring and reporting of military expenditures. The study strongly recommended the continuous use of the reporting instrument by an ever-increasing number of States, with the objective of universal participation. That would permit a better assessment of its general usefulness and viability, while facilitating the conclusion of verifiable agreements on the reduction of military expenditures in the future.

The Western countries have generally supported the efforts described above for the improvement and wider use of the reporting instrument, while the Soviet Union and its allies have insisted on the need for political decisions that would facilitate early negotiations for agreement on reductions of military budgets rather than for study which, they have held, would only serve to delay action. At the 1982 special session devoted to disarmament, the President of the United States proposed the establishment of an international conference on military expenditures to build on the work of the United Nations. The Soviet Union, however, has maintained its objections to that approach, affirming that what is needed are concrete moves towards the freezing and actual reduction of military expenditures, in either percentages or absolute terms, and that continuing polemics on the issue constitute a digression from the substance of the question.

Every year since 1979 the General Assembly, at the initiative of Romania, has adopted a resolution on the reduction of military budgets. It has requested the Disarmament Commission to continue the consideration of this issue in order to harmonize views and identify and elaborate the principles which should govern further actions of States in the field of freezing and reducing military expenditure. The Commission might then, if appropriate, embody such principles in a suitable document.

Also every year since 1980, at the initiative of Sweden, the Assembly has adopted resolutions dealing with the question of developing and universalizing, through further studies and surveys, the international system for the measurement and the reporting of military expenditures. These resolutions have led to a number of the reports and exercises considered above.

The General Assembly, in its resolution 37/95 B of December 1982, requested the Secretary-General, with the assistance of a group of qualified experts and with the voluntary co-operation of States, to undertake the task of constructing price indices and purchasing-power parities for military expenditures of participating States and to submit progress reports to the Assembly at its 1983 and 1984 sessions and a final report in 1985. This task should encompass a study of the problem as a whole, which would include the following:

(a) To assess the feasibility of such an exercise;

(b) To design the project and methodology to be employed;

(c) To determine the types of data required;

(d) To construct military price indices and purchasing-power parities.

Despite progress made on the reporting system itself, the basic differences in approach to the problem of reducing military budgets remain. On the one hand, several States, mainly the Soviet Union and other Eastern European States, believe that a political decision, followed by substantive negotiations, would provide an early solution. They maintain that expert studies serve mainly to delay such a political solution. On the other hand, Western and other countries emphasize the necessity of first solving the technical issues of establishing an adequate, verifiable comparison of the various States' expenditures, which would serve as a basis for the negotiation of agreements on their reduction. Still others, particularly developing countries, stress the allocation of enormous resources on arms when two thirds of humanity lives in hunger and poverty. They regret the lack of political will to reduce arms and military expenditures, and regard the study of technical issues as useful, but feel that it should not delay progress on actual reductions to aid both disarmament and development.

Chapter XIII

The World Disarmament Campaign and the role of public opinion

The concept of the global dissemination of factual and objective information to the general public is not new to the United Nations. The positive role and importance of well-informed public opinion was repeatedly acknowledged by the General Assembly as a natural consequence of an Organization whose Charter is prefaced with the words: "We the peoples of the United Nations determined to save succeeding generations from the scourge of war". Already at its first session, in 1946, the Assembly recognized that "the United Nations cannot achieve the purposes for which it has been created unless the peoples of the world are fully informed of its aims and activities".

The role of world public opinion in promoting specifically the cause of disarmament was fully recognized in 1978 at the first special session of the General Assembly devoted to disarmament. For the first time in the history of the Organization the Assembly gave leading representatives of non-governmental organizations (NGOs) the opportunity to address it and to submit their views in writing. The Final Document, adopted by consensus at the end of the special session, recognized the importance of the potential role of public opinion in supporting disarmament efforts and initiated a new phase of United Nations efforts directed towards that end. In particular, the Final Document stated that "it is essential that not only Governments but also the peoples of the world recognize and understand the dangers" of the arms race. In view of this, the General Assembly, in the Final Document, called upon Member States, governmental and non-governmental organizations and the United Nations and its specialized agencies to increase their information activities with regard to the danger represented by the armaments race and with regard to the efforts to achieve disarmament "in order that an international conscience may develop and that world public opinion may exercise a positive influence".

The Final Document, furthermore, proclaimed the week starting 24 October, the day of the foundation of the United Nations, as a week devoted to fostering the objective of disarmament. It envisaged special activities for the Week, including efforts of Governments, United Nations bodies, research institutes, educational institutions, the information media and other non-governmental organizations. Disarmament Week was conceived as an annual event to reach out to ever-greater numbers of people in every country and to increase their understanding of the issues involved in arms limitation and disarmament. The Secretary-General was requested to report to the Assembly on the world-wide observance of the Week, including the information received from Member States on their respective national activities.

In line with the decisions of the special session, the then Centre for Disarmament (now the Department for Disarmament Affairs), together with the Department of Public Information and specialized agencies, in particular UNESCO, was given an important role in the production and dissemination of information material on disarmament.

For its part, the Centre intensified a number of its activities. Thus, contacts with non-governmental organizations interested in disarmament were strengthened and deepened. In the area of publications, besides *The United Nations Disarmament Yearbook*, the Centre initiated and expanded production of a variety of materials on disarmament for wide distribution. For instance, it developed the Study Series on various substantive issues and provided wider distribution to publications such as the Fact Sheets and the periodical *Disarmament*. The Centre also intensified its participation in various intergovernmental and non-governmental conferences and seminars and it started organizing regional seminars for non-governmental constituencies. The Department of Public Information, for its part, increased its disarmament-related information activities at Headquarters and in the field.

In 1980, in order to find ways and means of increasing public awareness of arms limitation and disarmament issues, the General Assembly, on the initiative of Mexico, adopted a resolution by which it requested the Secretary-General to undertake a study on the organization and financing of a world disarmament campaign under the auspices of the United Nations.

The Secretary-General's report entitled "World Disarmament Campaign", submitted to the Assembly in 1981, stated that the general purpose of the campaign should be to inform, to educate and to generate public understanding and support for the objectives of the United Nations in the field of arms limitation and disarmament. It also indicated that a continuing co-operative effort would be required from the United Nations system, Member States and a wide range of governmental and non-governmental organizations.

The General Assembly commended the study and decided to transmit it, along with views of Member States concerning it, to the Assembly at its second special session devoted to disarmament, in 1982, for the solemn launching of the Campaign.

The World Disarmament Campaign was in fact launched at the opening meeting of the second special session, on 7 June 1982. Four days later, the Secretary-General submitted to the Assembly an outline of a programme for the Campaign, which was discussed in the course of the session.

In the general debate, Member States, while expressing support for the World Disarmament Campaign, stressed the need for a balanced, impartial and objective approach to it and also emphasized that it was important for the non-governmental organizations to play an active role. Some States voiced their concern as to whether the people in all countries would have free access to information about the arms race and disarmament, as well as to what extent their views would bear effectively on the disarmament policies of their respective Governments.

As a result of intense efforts in various bodies, the special session was able to reach consensus on a text describing the World Disarmament Campaign. In the agreed text, the objectives, contents and modalities of the Campaign were defined, as discussed below. The Secretary-General was requested to submit to the 1982 regular session of the General Assembly a report outlining the general framework for, and providing the specifics of, a programme of activities for 1983, together with its financial aspects. In addition, he was requested to submit to each subsequent regular session of the Assembly, for its review, a report on the implementation of the Campaign during the preceding year and to convey to the Assembly the relevant views of the Advisory Board on Disarmament Studies.

At its regular session in 1982, the General Assembly adopted three resolutions on the World Disarmament Campaign. One, introduced by Mexico, was adopted by consensus. It approved the general framework and the 1983 programme of activities for the Campaign, as proposed in the Secretary-General's report, invited Member States that had not yet done so to supplement available United Nations resources with voluntary contributions, declared that voluntary donations by non-governmental organizations, foundations, trusts and other private sources would also be welcome and decided that at its next session there should be a pledging conference of contributions of Member States for the World Disarmament Campaign.

The second resolution, initiated by the United States, was also adopted by consensus. It recognized that well-informed discussion on all points of view on disarmament issues might have a positive influence on the attainment of progress in disarmament, and expressed the conviction that the best way to build trust and confidence and to advance the conditions which could contribute to disarmament was through the co-operation and participation of all States and by the widest dissemination of information and unimpeded access for all sectors of the public to a broad range of information and opinion concerning disarmament. The resolution called on Member States to further the objectives of the World Disarmament Campaign and to encourage their citizens to express freely and publicly their views on disarmament questions and to organize and meet publicly for that purpose.

The third resolution, introduced by Bulgaria and adopted by a vote, invited Member States, in implementing the World Disarmament Campaign, to take into account Bulgaria's proposal for launching world-wide action for collecting signatures in support of measures to prevent nuclear war, to curb the arms race and for disarmament, and also to co-operate with the United Nations to ensure a better flow of information on the various aspects of disarmament. The three Western nuclear Powers abstained on that particular resolution.

The following year, in 1983, the General Assembly adopted two further resolutions. The one, sponsored by Mexico, was along the lines of the previous year's and was adopted by consensus. It approved the Secretary-General's report on the programme of activities and decided on the holding of a second pledging conference in 1984. The other resolution, sponsored again by Bulgaria and adopted by a vote, was similar in nature to the 1982 initiative.

In the course of the 1984 session, the General Assembly adopted several resolutions dealing with the World Disarmament Campaign.

The resolution sponsored by Bulgaria and other socialist countries requested that wider publicity be given to the General Assembly's work in disarmament and especially to proposals of Member States and action taken on them. The resolution was adopted by a vote of 117 to none, with 31 abstentions.

By the resolution sponsored by Mexico and eight non-aligned and neutral countries and, later, by Romania, the General Assembly decided that there should be a third pledging conference at the fortieth session of the General Assembly. The resolution expressed the hope that Member States that had not yet announced any voluntary contributions to the Trust Fund of the World Disarmament Campaign might do so. It was then adopted by a vote of 124 to none, with 12 abstentions.

A resolution introduced by Togo on behalf of several African and other non-aligned countries was adopted without a vote. By that resolution, the Secretary-General was both requested to provide assistance to such Member States in the regions concerned as might request it with a view to establishing regional and institutional arrangements for the implementation of the World Disarmament Campaign and to report to the General Assembly on the issue at its fortieth session.

General framework of the Campaign

The World Disarmament Campaign has three primary purposes: to inform, to educate and to generate public understanding and support for the objectives of the United Nations in the field of arms limitation and disarmament.

The Campaign is carried out in all regions of the world in a balanced, factual and objective manner. Its universality is to be guaranteed by the co-operation and participation of all States and by the widest possible dissemination of information and unimpeded access for all sectors of the public to a broad range of information and opinions on questions of arms limitation and disarmament and the dangers relating to all aspects of the arms race and war, in particular nuclear war.

Member States are encouraged to co-operate with the United Nations to ensure a better flow of information with regard to the various aspects of disarmament and to avoid dissemination of false and tendentious information. In carrying out the Campaign, emphasis is to be placed on the relationship between disarmament and international security and between disarmament and development, given the benefits that could be derived from the reduction of military outlays and the reallocation of released resources for socio-economic development. In this regard, the Campaign provides an opportunity for discussion and debate in all countries on all points of view relating to the question of disarmament, its objectives and conditions. The Campaign also encourages bilateral and multilateral exchanges on the basis of reciprocity and mutual agreement and gives the widest possible dissemination to such exchanges, for example, among government officials, experts, academicians and journalists of different countries.

The United Nations provides information for and generally co-ordinates the implementation of the World Disarmament Campaign, which is carried out at the global, regional and national level under its auspices.

In addition, the Campaign is designed to facilitate and complement existing programmes of information, research, education and training in the area of disarmament. The promotion of such programmes is encouraged, particularly in the developing countries, and the United Nations and its agencies are instrumental in this process.

The United Nations information and education activities, conducted in accordance with the purposes and principles of the Charter of the United Nations, must be global in scope and content and use those means of communication which are most appropriate in reaching the largest number of people. Although the means of informing and educating may vary from region to region, the basic thrust of the activities for the Campaign should be equally effective in all regions of the world.

Every effort is made to ensure an equitable and timely distribution of materials in accordance with the principle of conducting the Campaign on a universal basis. In this regard, the United Nations information centres and field offices play a key role.

The Campaign makes use of all available means of communication and fully utilizes the mass media, since they provide the most effective means of gaining access to the public and promoting a climate of understanding, confidence and co-operation conducive to peace and disarmament.

ACTORS IN THE CAMPAIGN

There are three major "actors" in achieving the objectives of the Campaign: the United Nations system, Member States and non-governmental organizations.

The United Nations system is, in itself, a major source of initiatives, materials, co-ordination and guidance in the conduct of the Campaign. In particular, the United Nations must stimulate the efforts of Governments and non-governmental organizations and support them by providing and disseminating, in all countries and regions of the world, factual, balanced and objective information on relevant disarmament issues. It must also publicize, as effectively and as widely as possible, the activities of the Campaign. However, the United Nations system should not be expected to endorse, direct or substitute for the activities of Campaign constituencies in the field of disarmament.

The success of the Campaign depends to a great extent on the active and material support of Member States. Indeed, there are several areas in which States can contribute, and have already done so, to its effectiveness, for instance:

— In assisting the United Nations in disseminating factual and objective information with regard to the various aspects of the arms race and disarmament;

— In helping to publicize the Campaign among all sectors of the public and thereby making it better known worldwide as a programme of the United Nations;

— In co-operating with the United Nations in the organization of regional seminars and conferences;

— In producing the United Nations disarmament information materials in languages other than the six official languages of the Organization.

Furthermore, Member States can provide material support to the Campaign by pledging contributions to its Voluntary Trust Fund.

Non-governmental organizations have traditionally promoted the purposes and principles of the Charter of the United Nations and have actively supported the work of the Organization. In the field of disarmament and peace, the non-governmental organizations have acted as effective disseminators of information generated by the United Nations and have offered Member States and the United Nations system their opinions and expertise.

The 1978 and 1982 special sessions of the General Assembly provided important occasions for the participation of non-governmental organizations. Representatives of 25 non-governmental organizations and 6 research institutes spoke at the first special session. In 1982, as many as 53 non-governmental organizations and 23 research institutes participated, reflecting an increasing public awareness of the dangers of the arms race.

In December 1983, for the first time, and in December 1984, the Advisory Board on Disarmament Studies, which, among other functions, advises the Secretary-General on the implementation of the World Disarmament Campaign, invited representatives of the Non-governmental Organizations Committee on Disarmament at United Nations Headquarters, the Special NGO (non-governmental organizations) Committee on Disarmament at Geneva and the World Federation of United Nations Associations to contribute to its work by presenting the views of their organizations on the Campaign. Another such meeting is planned for 1985.

The involvement of non-governmental organizations in the Campaign began in 1981 when the Group of Experts which was to prepare the Secretary-General's report on the organization and financing of a world disarmament campaign, sent a questionnaire to non-governmental organizations around the world, seeking their views on various aspects of the subject. In addition, a representative of the non-governmental organizations' community acted as a consultant to the experts throughout their work. Since the official launching of the Campaign, frequent consultations on its implementation have taken place between the United Nations and non-governmental organizations.

CONSTITUENCIES

The World Disarmament Campaign is directed to all segments of the world's population. However, in order to achieve a higher degree of effectiveness, certain groups and professions have been singled out for particular attention because of their special influence and multiplier effect on society. They fall into five major categories: elected representatives, non-governmental organizations, the media, educational institutions and research institutes.

Elected representatives, parliamentarians and public officials have a direct impact upon policy-making processes of Member States. Their involvement in the Campaign can be highly beneficial, as they are in a position to encourage continuing debate of disarmament issues in governmental and parliamentary circles and to assist in generating support for the Campaign.

Both national and international non-governmental organizations have a fundamental role in the World Disarmament Campaign. The non-governmental organizations' community is representative of a wide range of categories and occupations; it is also in a position to reach a growing number of people with the most diverse backgrounds and interests.

The media are organized disseminators of information and are capable of effectively reaching millions of people throughout the world. The educational community can play an important role in helping to create well-informed public opinion in favour of disarmament. Research institutes also contribute to the objectives of the World Disarmament Campaign, particularly by providing in-depth information on various aspects of disarmament and the arms race.

Co-ordination

The Department for Disarmament Affairs has been designated by the General Assembly as the overall co-ordinator of the World Disarmament Campaign. It is responsible for co-ordinating Campaign activities within the United Nations system and for maintaining liaison with governmental and non-governmental organizations and research institutes.

The Department of Public Information, in view of its specific mandate in the field of public information, plays an important role in the fulfilment of the objectives of the Campaign, particularly in carrying out a wide range of public information activities and in utilizing its expertise and resources to ensure the Campaign's maximum effectiveness.

The United Nations information centres play a key role in enlisting support for disarmament at the regional and subregional levels and are actively involved in carrying out the World Disarmament Campaign at the local level. They give the widest possible dissemination to the materials for distribution.

Specialized agencies and subsidiary organs of the United Nations have also been encouraged to contribute to the Campaign in their specific areas of concern and expertise.

In order to fulfil its responsibilities, the Department for Disarmament Affairs maintains close liaison with all relevant departments of the United Nations Secretariat and with the specialized agencies, non-governmental organizations, research institutes and educational institutions. Consultations are held on a regular basis with a view to sharing information on the implementation of the Campaign and identifying the most effective ways in which activities can be organized and carried out.

The Advisory Board on Disarmament Studies also has a role to play in the co-ordination of the Campaign. The Board is composed of a group of eminent persons from various parts of the world who are invited by the Secretary-General to advise him on specific disarmament research and studies matters. Among its other functions, the Board provides the Secretary-General with recommendations each year on the implementation of the World Disarmament Campaign. Since 1983, the Advisory

Board has met with representatives of non-governmental organizations active in the field of disarmament.

FINANCE

The World Disarmament Campaign is financed from within existing United Nations resources, supplemented by voluntary contributions from Member States and private sources. Thus, the success of the Campaign depends in large measure upon the extent of the active and material support of Member States, especially upon their extrabudgetary contributions. To that end, the Secretary-General, in 1982, established a voluntary trust fund, and, as of March 1985, a total of 42 countries have made pledges to the Fund, totalling approximately $3.4 million, most of it in non-convertible currencies. In addition, in the course of the past three years, a number of private sources also contributed to the Fund.

The countries that have contributed so far are: Australia, Austria, Bangladesh, Bulgaria, Burma, Byelorussian SSR, Cameroon, Canada, China, Cuba, Czechoslovakia, Democratic Yemen, Denmark, Egypt, Finland, German Democratic Republic, Greece, Hungary, India (two pledges), Indonesia, Iraq, Ireland, Japan, Kuwait, Lao People's Democratic Republic, Libyan Arab Jamahiriya, Mexico, Mongolia, New Zealand, Nigeria, Norway, Pakistan, Poland, Romania, Sri Lanka, Sweden, Tunisia, Uganda, Ukrainian SSR, USSR, Viet Nam and Yugoslavia.

The next pledging conference is scheduled for October 1985 during Disarmament Week.

Programme of activities of the Campaign

A wide range of activities have been envisaged for the United Nations in implementing the Campaign. They can be grouped into five major areas: (*a*) preparation and dissemination of materials; (*b*) conferences, seminars and training; (*c*) special events; (*d*) a publicity programme; and (*e*) services of United Nations field offices.

UNITED NATIONS INFORMATION MATERIALS

The first category of activities aims at the promotion of "the widest possible dissemination of information and unimpeded access for all sectors of the public to a broad range of information and opinions on the questions of arms limitation and disarmament".

Since the Campaign was launched, both the production and the distribution of United Nations disarmament information materials have gradually increased, and a further expansion is envisaged in the coming years. Materials include recurrent United Nations publications, such as *The United Nations Disarmament Yearbook*, the periodical *Disarmament*, the Studies Series and Fact Sheets on various current topics. The World Disarmament Campaign "Newsletter", educational kits and booklets and leaflets on specific issues provide easy access to information on the progress of the Campaign and on efforts within the United Nations to achieve disarmament.

The audio-visual information materials include posters, wallsheets, sets of slides, films, exhibits and radio and television programmes, such as the forthcoming programme under the *Agenda for a Small Planet* series, which will bring together some 20 television producers from different regions of the world, each of them producing a film on a disarmament issue.

CONFERENCES, SEMINARS AND TRAINING

This category of activities includes meetings, lectures, conferences and consultations between the United Nations and target constituencies of the Campaign. The purpose is to inform and educate audiences and thereby further increase understanding of and commitment to the goals of disarmament.

Such events have already been held in Mexico, Kenya, Thailand, Romania, India, Venezuela, the USSR, Egypt and Sweden, and others are being planned. Invitations to attend these meetings are extended to all five major constituencies of the Campaign so that they can interact and exchange views on how best to further understanding and support for the objectives of the United Nations in the field of disarmament. In addition, seminars and training programmes specifically geared to a single constituency of the Campaign are also organized, bearing in mind its particular characteristics. For example, there have been round-tables for mass-media leaders, training programmes for young journalists and broadcasters and seminars for educators.

Disarmament internship programmes for graduate students are also part of this category of activity. Two such programmes are currently carried out: the first, developed in co-operation with the United Nations *ad hoc* internship programme, extends throughout the entire year; the second takes place in the summer, in co-operation with the graduate student intern programme of the Department of Public Information.

The programme of fellowships on disarmament for young public officials from different countries also helps further the aims of the Campaign.

SPECIAL EVENTS

Special events offer additional opportunities to increase public awareness of the danger of the arms race and to create an atmosphere conducive to progress in disarmament. Disarmament Week, from 24 to 31 October, is one such event and is celebrated at United Nations Headquarters and worldwide with increasing non-governmental participation.

The United Nations information centres and other field offices have a highly important role in motivating, throughout the world, the constituencies of the Campaign to take an active part in their observance of Disarmament Week.

A publicity programme for the World Disarmament Campaign itself is an additional means of implementing the Campaign. It is carried out in close contact with the press and the media in general, with growing involvement of non-governmental organizations and through the support of well-known personalities in the arts and sciences, in sports and in public affairs.

UNITED NATIONS FIELD OFFICES

United Nations information centres and field offices have an important role in initiating and supporting local activities within the World Disarmament Campaign. They disseminate substantive information, enlist the co-operation of local non-governmental organizations for the Campaign, provide assistance in the organization of regional seminars and conferences, promote the publication of United Nations disarmament information materials in local languages, organize exhibits, prepare special briefings and seminars for journalists and other audiences and participate in events organized by Governments.

The future

The World Disarmament Campaign can be conducted effectively only if it is based on co-operation and interaction between the United Nations, Member States and governmental and non-governmental organizations. Its effectiveness increases with the degree of such co-operation and interaction. In evaluating the way in which the Campaign is implemented, one must bear in mind its nature. The purpose of the Campaign is to stimulate, in an objective and factual way, world-wide public interest in, and support for, disarmament and to promote awareness of the situation and the problems involved.

Within that general framework, the United Nations has a specific role to play. At this stage, however, it cannot direct or substitute for the efforts of non-governmental organizations and other bodies. Nor can the United Nations endorse or disapprove of various activities in different regions of the world. The guidelines for the Campaign, laid down by the General Assembly, make it clear that it is to be an effort in which Governments, non-governmental organizations and the United Nations each have complementary roles. The role of the United Nations, in particular, is to be a major source of initiative and guidance in the conduct of the Campaign and to stimulate and support efforts by providing and disseminating in all countries, in all regions of the world, factual and objective information on relevant subjects, and to publicize the activities of the Campaign itself as widely as possible. If, in doing so, the Organization contributes to the success of the Campaign, thus furthering solid progress towards real measures of arms limitation and disarmament, it will have accomplished a great deal.

Department for Disarmament Affairs
Co-ordination and World Disarmament Campaign Section
United Nations, Room 3161
New York, NY 10017

DPI/864

Printed in U.S.A.   C 02295   United Nations publication
40883—November 1985—17,000   P 01695   Sales No. E.85.IX.6
                                              ISBN 92-1-142112-8